THE MASTER TELLS STORIES

THE MASTER TELLS STORIES

BY MASTER CHENG YEN

TRANSLATED BY LIN SEN-SHOU

Still Thoughts Cultural Mission Co., Ltd.

The Master Tells Stories

Published by the Still Thoughts Cultural Mission Co., Ltd.
Foreign Language Publications Department
1st Fl., No. 19, Alley 7, Lane 217,
Chunghsiao E. Road, Sec. 3, Taipei, Taiwan, Rep. of China
Telephone: 886-2-776-0111
Fax: 886-2-776-0514
E-mail: kpliu@cc.tccm.edu.tw

Publisher: Shih Cheng Yen
Director of Tzu Chi Cultural Mission: Wang Tuan-cheng
Editor-in-chief: Liu King-pong
Translation by Lin Sen-shou
English editing and layout by Douglas Shaw
Cover painting by Mi Hsiung, Hung Kuan Buddhist Arts Center
Inside art by Hsiao Tzung-ren

ISBN 957-8444-16-8

CONTENTS

SECTION 1: BUDDHA AND HIS DISCIPLES

SECTION 2: SAVING LIVES FROM THIS VULGAR WORLD

SECTION 3: THE RESULTS OF KARMA

SECTION 4: THE PATH OF THE BODHISATTVAS

Section 1
BUDDHA AND
HIS DISCIPLES

Buddha taught us to follow the Path of the Bodhisattvas. We must become actively involved in society to put the spirit of Buddhism into practice. Those who can give selflessly are the happiest people.

Maudgalyayana Rescues His Mother

n India, between April and July, storms sweep in from the ocean, bringing wind and rain. Water is everywhere, but these heavy rains are necessary to nourish plants for the next growing season. In Buddha's time, monks traveled on foot, but during the rainy season this became all but impossible because of the water everywhere. Also, Buddha didn't want his monks to accidentally step on the tender young plants pushing up through the earth or any of the tiny insects that flourished in this weather. For these reasons, Buddha declared the rainy season to be a time of retreat. The monks gathered in one place, usually in a grove of trees to help protect them from the torrents of rain, and they used this time to study or to meditate.

One day during the summer retreat, the monk Maudgalyayana was meditating, He suddenly remembered his mother, who had died many years before. He loved her very much, but he also knew that she hadn't been a good person. Her life had been full of what Buddha called the "three poisons": greed, anger and delusion. His mother had been very greedy. She was always willing to cheat or trick someone in order to get a bit more for herself. Her heart was full of anger, and she often scolded or cursed others, especially when things didn't go her way. And of course, she didn't see how poor her spiritual life was, how impermanent the material things she so eagerly sought were, and how her actions would only lead to more suffering.

Knowing what kind of person his mother had been, Maudgalyayana was worried about where she might go in her next life. Of all Buddha's disciples, Maudgalyayana had the strongest powers of concentration, gained through long hours of sitting in meditation. He could do things that no one else could do. So he entered deeply into meditation, and he saw that she was in a dreadful place: hell.

There he saw those who had done wrong in their lives and the punishments they received. He felt sorry for them, because they were in so much agony. When he entered the realm of hungry ghosts, Maudgalyayana saw people who were suffering from their greediness in their previous lives. Their bellies were big and round, swollen with hunger, but their mouths were tiny, no bigger than the eye of a needle. Their arms and legs were weak, and their eyes were wide open with hunger. The ghosts were all starving and they howled in pain. The sight was so horrible that Maudgalyayana could hardly bear to look at it.

Then he suddenly saw the person he had been thinking of all along—his mother. She looked like all the other hungry ghosts and tears covered her face. Hunger burned inside her stomach. Maudgalyayana was in pain just from watching her. He asked her about her agony. "I'm starving," she replied. "I have no water or food. There is a fire burning in me and I need water and food!"

Maudgalyayana was said to have the greatest supernatural powers among Buddha's disciples. Now his mother needed water and food, and this was very easy for him! So he used his magical powers and a bowl of rice and a cup of water appeared. He gave them to her and she was very excited. Although her hands were weak, she still held out her hands at once to receive them. Enduring the pain and the shaking of her body, she brought them close to her mouth. When the water and rice had just barely touched her lips, a ball of fire suddenly shot from her mouth. The water evaporated and the rice was burnt.

Maudgalyayana felt as though a knife had just stabbed him in the heart, and he didn't know what to do. Although he had many magical powers, his mother had so much bad karma that he was powerless to help her. Full of despair, he came out of his meditation.

Back again in the grove of trees, Maudgalyayana stood up and walked to where Buddha was preaching to a small group of disciples. As always, he reverently bowed low before Buddha, feeling his great compassion and wisdom. He felt that Buddha would be willing to help, even though his mother had done many evil things in her life. He explained what he had seen and Buddha listened carefully. At the end of his tale, Maudgalyayana asked Buddha why he couldn't save his mother. "What did she do that made her go to hell? What should I do to save her?"

"Each one of us always suffers the results of our actions," Buddha replied kindly. "When your mother was alive, she planted the seeds of greed, anger and delusion. She was greedy for other people's hard labor and money and thus planted the seed of greed. She was also hostile and ignorant. She didn't praise others, but lied about them instead. The anger in her mind was very powerful. When she was alive, she didn't respect Buddhism or the goal of spiritual development. This kind of ignorance keeps her from being saved. She has to accept her bad karma. Her bad karma has piled up as high as a mountain, and your powers are not enough to save her."

When Maudgalyayana heard this, he felt disheartened. Still he asked Buddha to help him rescue her. Buddha was touched by his disciple's love for his mother. "In order to save her, you need more than your own strength, because your mother's karmic obstacles are too great. In this grove of trees, there are many holy monks whose minds are pure and whose good deeds have helped them accumulate much merit. If you gather these monks together and give all their merit to your mother, she will surely be saved from her fate in hell."

"You should also try to create merit on her behalf," Buddha continued. "On the fifteenth day of the seventh month, the last day of the summer retreat, you must offer food to these monks and thus plant seeds of goodness. Then all of you must pray for your mother with pure, joyful hearts. The resulting strength, and only this strength, will be able to transform her bad karma."

When Maudgalyayana heard this, he was exultant. Following Buddha's advice, he went to each honorable monk in turn. Before each, he bowed reverently and asked for his help in rescuing his mother. Naturally, the monks all agreed to help.

At the end of the rainy season retreat, Maudgalyayana prepared a lot of vegetarian dishes. He offered a bowl of clean water to each monk for him to wash his hands (because the Indians ate with their bare hands), and he

offered them food with utmost sincerity. Then all the
monks gathered their strength and prayed for his mother.
They dedicated the merit from their religious works to
Maudgalyayana's mother, and the strength of their merit
was unbelievable.

That evening, as Maudgalyayana sat in meditation, he saw a celestial woman floating towards
him. She bowed before him, and as he looked
close, he saw that this woman was his mother. She
thanked him, saying, "Because of your power and filial
heart, because of the merit of those many venerable
monks, and also because of Buddha's compassion, I have
been released from the realm of hungry ghosts and ele-
vated to the realm of the heavens."

Maudgalyayana was delighted to hear this. After his
meditation was finished, he immediately went and bowed
reverently before Buddha and all the monks in thanks for
their assistance.

The Pregnant Nun

Within the Buddhist community, there was a woman who came from a rich family in Rajagrha. In her childhood, she was very intelligent, and she was never interested in the beautiful clothes and ornaments that other girls adored. Her mind was always calm and she was unusually wise for a child. Intuitively, she sensed that everything in this world changes and passes away very quickly. At a young age, she thought of becoming a nun in order to search for the Truth.

When she was old enough, her parents married her off to a wealthy, cultured young man in the city. She had a wonderful life and her husband treated her well. In spite of her husband's wealth, she still lived a simple, frugal life. At this time, she was already pregnant, but she didn't know it.

One day, the city threw a huge celebration. It was a very important festival, and the city was extravagantly decorated. There was an atmosphere of excitement, and all the people were decked out in their most elegant clothes. "You always wear plain clothes and never put on any makeup," her husband observed. "But today's a big day, so you should get dressed up."

"What's the use?" she replied to his surprise. "A person's body is full of filth. Our life slips through our fingers as we quickly approach death. When we die, our body will simply rot and stink. Decorating the body is like spraying perfume on a toilet. What's the use?" When her husband heard this, he felt confused, with hate and love mixed up together. He retorted, "If that's so, why don't you just become a nun?" She was delighted. "Oh, thank you very much! That's just what I've always wanted! If you can help me to accomplish my wish, then you too will receive boundless merit."

Her husband didn't understand her conviction, and he regretted having spoken so thoughtlessly. He kept trying to persuade her to change her mind, but her mind was made up and she was determined to become a nun. Although he didn't want to part with her, he had no choice but to let her go. He ordered a number of servants, laden down with various boxes and trunks full of things he thought she would need, to accompany her. With this entourage, she went to a religious group to become a nun.

At last she had achieved her wish to lead a religious life, and she was very happy. However, she still didn't know about the child growing inside her. Her belly slowly increased in size. "Are you pregnant?" people asked her. "You look like you are." She didn't know how to respond. Someone brought her to see Devadatta, the leader of this religious group. He was son of King Dronodana and a cousin of Sakyamuni Buddha. He was also Buddha's enemy and rival. He only wanted to learn magical powers and to replace Buddha as the new religious leader. When Devadatta saw her, he was angry. "How can there be a pregnant nun in my group? This will destroy my reputation." Without allowing her to defend herself, he expelled her from the group. She knew Devadatta's teaching wasn't what she was after, so she stood up, bowed to him and prepared to leave.

She begged another nun, who had expressed her sympathy, to go with her. "The assembly I want to join is not Devadatta's, but Buddha's. Will you go with me?" The nun walked with her to the place where Buddha was staying with his disciples.

When Buddha found out that she came from Devadatta's group, he thought, "If I accept her, there will certainly be rumors that I accepted those that Devadatta rejected. But all lives are equal and I should give her a chance for spiritual formation." Buddha decided to clear up this matter, not only to return her innocence, but also to establish the truth of the situation.

So he invited the king, his ministers, and the local laity. Buddha asked his disciple Upali to be in charge of this affair, because Upali was considered to be the most excellent in upholding the religious rules of the community.

When the king, the ministers and the laity had arrived, Upali asked a woman of good repute to question the young nun. "I want you to take this nun to a tent and ask her when she was married and when she left home. If she got pregnant when she was married, then she's innocent. Otherwise, she isn't. So you must ask her carefully."

This woman questioned the young woman carefully, and even examined her belly. The woman determined that the young woman had gotten pregnant when she was married and thus was innocent. This was happily announced to the assembly. Now the truth was known, and Buddha allowed her to stay in a house to wait for the birth. Several months later, she gave birth to an adorable boy.

ne day, the king was walking past the nunnery and heard a baby crying. He asked, "Why is there a baby crying in a nunnery?"

His attendant replied, "Your Majesty, don't you remember the gathering months ago that Buddha called? That nun has given birth to a boy."

The king was delighted to hear this news, but he wondered how a nun could bring up a child in a convent. So he took the child to a relative of his and named him Kumara. He also gave the boy the title of prince, so many people called him Prince Kumara. When he was seven years old, the king brought him back to the Buddhist assembly to begin his spiritual training.

The child was very smart and could speak very well. He was raised in the assembly, so his behavior and learning were exceptional. He was a good student. He saw all sorts of things and thought hard, trying to understand them. He meditated and became enlightened. His mother also became a meritorious nun, and they both served as good examples to all those who had spiritual aspirations.

We can see from this story that Buddha's wisdom and compassion embrace all beings. Instead of judging the situation hastily, Buddha analyzed matters to prove the young woman's innocence. She thus became a nun without a stain on her reputation. This was Buddha's compassion and wisdom in action. In comparison, Devadatta was much inferior.

Sariputra Sleeps Outdoors

ne time, King Anathapindita from Sravasti asked Buddha to preach in Rajagrha, and Buddha gladly accepted the invitation. The only road from Rajagrha to Sravasti ran north from Rajagrha. Buddha and his companions followed this road, crossing the Ganges river by boat. They continued north through Mt. Sumeru and its dangerous mountain ranges (now called the Himalayas). Then they turned to the west and walked for days to reach Sravasti.

Several days into their journey, one disciple came to Buddha and said, "Buddha, every one of us is tired and we won't reach Sravasti today. Can we spend the night at that hut over there?" Buddha agreed and the group turned toward the small house. When they got there, the monks were very excited. They had been sleeping outside on the ground for days, with rocks poking them in the back and insects buzzing in their ears. Their feet were sore and their legs ached. They were happy to sleep inside and be comfortable for a night. All the monks bustled about, arranging their belongings and stretching out for a long rest.

In India, it's very hot in the daytime, but cold at night. Buddha slept until midnight, but then became chilled. He sat up and suddenly sneezed. Someone outside also sneezed. Curious, he went out and saw a person under a tree. He asked, "Who is it?"

The person under the tree replied, "Buddha, it's me, Sariputra."

"Why are you out there?"

"When we arrived at the hut last night, everyone was busy finding a place to sleep. It was too crowded and I couldn't find a place, so I came out and stayed under this tree."

The next morning, Buddha gathered the disciples around. "Why did you rush around like that last night? We should all respect each other. Do you know who among all of you has the right to sit at the first seat, who can drink first, and who can accept the first offering?"

The monks were too young and inexperienced to answer thoughtfully. They all gave different answers. One said, "The ones with royal blood should sit at the first seats, because their status is higher, and they should drink and accept the offerings first."

Another said, "No, it should be those from the priestly class, because their status is superior, and after they become monks, we should all respect them more. We should let them sit in the best seats and drink and accept the offerings first."

Someone else said, "It should be the ones with supernatural powers!"

Buddha told them all to listen carefully. "When you learn from me, you all get the same instruction, so you must respect each other. Those who have just become monks must respect the older monks. They have been studying diligently and are more spiritually developed than you. They became monks earlier and started learning earlier than you. Their spiritual formation, behavior, conduct and merit are more developed, and so they're called 'senior monks.' All of you young monks must respect them."

After Buddha had finished, those young monks realized the purpose of this teaching. That night, they had been so tired that they just wanted to find a good spot to rest, without considering other people or respecting the senior monks. Thus Sariputra ended up under a tree, enduring the chill of the night. The young monks felt bad about being so discourteous, and they all went to apologize to Sariputra. From then on, they knew they had to respect each other, and they especially had to respect the older monks for their wisdom and learning. By respecting each other, all the monks got along very well together.

Buddha taught his disciples to turn away from evil, to follow goodness, to know who should be called "seniors," to know how to respect others, and to know how to be friendly. Following his teachings, Buddha's disciples learned how to control their thoughts and actions. They found that much of their suffering came from not thinking clearly and from acting in haste.

If each one of us can exercise a bit of self-control, our lives will be more enjoyable. We shouldn't ignore what seem to be small things in our daily lives. If we do, our minds won't be at ease. In short, we must start from the smallest things when we begin to learn Buddhism. For those who cultivate themselves mindfully, the Buddhist teachings can be found in their daily lives.

The Stubborn Snake

In Buddha's time, monks couldn't have any personal belongings, except for simple clothing and a bowl. In order to learn humility, they had to ask for food from both rich and poor families, and they had to accept gratefully whatever they were given, whether it was a delicious morsel or just a few grains of rice. The food of the day had to be finished that day, so that those generous offerings wouldn't go to waste. Also, no food was allowed after noon. Buddha also believed that his followers should only eat what was necessary, and that their noon meal provided them with enough energy to sustain them until the next day.

One morning, someone brought some especially delicious food to the monastery. At that time, the young monk who lived with Sariputra had already gone to the nearest village to ask for food. The food was equally divided among the monks present, and a bowl was also set aside for that other young monk.

As midday approached, the young monk still hadn't returned. Another monk came to Sariputra. "Senior, you prepared this bowl for the young monk, but it's almost noon. If you leave the food, it will be wasted. Why don't you just eat it yourself?" Sariputra thought this over and felt that eating the food was the right thing to do. When it passed midday, the food couldn't be eaten, and it would be wasteful and show ingratitude if he had to throw it away. So Sariputra ate the extra bowl of food.

Just as he finished eating, the young monk returned. "Oh, you're too late," Sariputra told him. "Someone gave us some delicious food, and I left a bowl for you. But at noon, you hadn't returned, so I had to eat it."

When the young monk heard this, he felt unhappy. He snapped, "If the food is tasty, people naturally like to eat a little extra."

When Sariputra heard this response, he was upset. He thought he had done the right thing so as not to waste the food. He declared, "From now on, I won't eat any food that requires chewing!" From that time on, he never ate food that he needed to chew, no matter whether it was morning or noon.

After a long time, everyone became quite worried about him and thought, "The Senior can't forget this incident. What should we do?" Buddha saw two or three monks talking to each other and asked them what they were discussing. One of them reported the incident to Buddha. "This is Sariputra's old habit," Buddha exclaimed, and he told them a story.

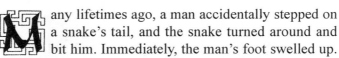 any lifetimes ago, a man accidentally stepped on a snake's tail, and the snake turned around and bit him. Immediately, the man's foot swelled up. His family was quite worried and asked a doctor to treat him. When the doctor saw the wound, he said that it had been caused by a poisonous snake and that there were two ways to treat it: they could catch the snake and force it to suck back the poison, or they could treat the wound with medicine. If they used medicine, the wound would take a long time to heal. The doctor let the family choose which method to use.

The family thought that forcing the snake to suck out the poison was the fastest way, so they had someone catch the snake. The doctor tried many ways to get the snake to suck out the poison, but the snake wouldn't do it. At last, they built a fire to force the snake to suck out the poison, but the snake crawled into the fire rather than suck back the poison. The doctor saw that the snake was determined not to suck back the poison and immediately took the snake away with a stick. He then applied medicine to the man's wound, and after a long course of treatment the man got better.

When Buddha finished the story, he explained it to the monks. "In our previous incarnations, that snake was Sariputra and I was the doctor. At that time, the snake stubbornly refused to change his mind, just as Sariputra now refuses to let go of that incident. A few words from the young monk made him insist that he wouldn't eat any food that had to be chewed. Isn't this the same habit he had lifetimes ago?"

Sariputra had acquired much wisdom and every word he said was meaningful, yet he still had the same old habit. People are often like this. When other people have their own problems, we happily give advice and think we can solve them, but we're unable to solve our own. Spiritual formation isn't only helping others to solve their problems, but is also being mindful of our own faults and bad habits. Learning to behave like Buddha means letting go of our attachments and not clinging to anything. Someone who does this is a true student of Buddhism, and the goal of becoming a buddha won't be far away.

Why Ananda Recited the Sutras

After Buddha passed away, his teachings were transmitted among his followers, but there were no tape recorders or pens and paper to record them. When a sermon was over, however, the sounds quickly faded into silence. Buddha's closest followers wanted to share Buddha's teachings with people, and they discussed how best to transmit the dharma. They decided that the teachings should be compiled into sutras, and many people nominated Ananda to be responsible for this task.

However, Ananda had not attained arhathood. Arhats are people who have achieved a very high degree of wisdom. Their karma is almost entirely cleansed, and at their death arhats pass into nirvana, never to be reincarnated again. During the meeting to discuss how to transmit the dharma, Mahakasyapa, a senior disciple, called Ananda in front of five hundred arhats and admonished him for having anxieties and an impure mind. Mahakasyapa declared that Ananda wasn't worthy of gathering with those who had achieved arhathood. Ananda humbled himself and begged the arhats for understanding, but they continued to criticize him.

One person reminded the audience that when Ananda was Buddha's attendant, he showed disrespect by stepping on Buddha's robe while folding it. "This is true," Ananda immediately responded. "But it happened because the wind blew the robe while I was folding it, and I accidentally stepped on it. It was unintentional, and I meant no disrespect to Buddha."

There came another criticism: when Buddha wanted a cup of water, why didn't Ananda rush to bring water to Buddha? "This is also true. When Buddha had a fever, he needed water. I took his bowl and ran quickly to the river-bank. Just as I bent to scoop up some water, some cattle suddenly rushed past and stirred up the river, making the water all muddy. I couldn't give Buddha dirty water! There was nothing I could do."

Another arhat raised a more serious criticism. "Ananda, it was also your fault that Buddha passed away early! When Buddha said to you, 'A buddha can live for 500 years or 80 years,' why didn't you ask Buddha to live longer? Why were you silent? Buddha said this three times, and if someone had requested him to stay, he could have lived for 500 years. You didn't ask him!"

"You're right," Ananda replied sadly. "Buddha once said that all creatures have many obstacles to overcome. If he had been asked to stay for 500 years, he could have done so, but my mind was blinded by ignorance. Although I wanted to open my mouth and beg Buddha to live for another 500 years, I just couldn't do it. I was very angry with myself." When Ananda said this, he was very sad and even wept. He regretted his mistakes very much and asked for forgiveness from everyone.

Mahakasyapa was not satisfied. "Ananda, from these incidents we know that your mind is still not tranquil. Too many emotions still sway your thoughts and actions. You should leave and develop your mind. You can return when your worries and ignorance are gone."

adly, Ananda returned to his own room. He did not blame the others, because he knew that when Buddha was alive, he didn't try hard enough to eliminate his anxieties and distractions. So Ananda threw himself into his studies. After seven days of continuous work, he was very tired and wanted to rest. At that very moment, his body felt very light and all of his anxieties disappeared. He felt full of radiance, and he experienced a kind of happiness that couldn't be described.

Joyfully, Ananda ran to the place where the arhats were gathered. He knocked on the door, but no one opened it for him. They told him to use his wisdom to enter, so he applied the powers that he had developed through meditation and entered the building. His mind was at peace, and he prostrated himself with appreciation and respect before all the arhats. He described his state of serenity to the others. Everyone was happy for him and asked him to recite what he had heard from Buddha.

Ananda then walked to the podium and began to recite. As he stood at the podium, his peaceful mind gave a new gracefulness and gentleness to his posture. There was a stir among the audience because Ananda's face was so radiant, and some of the arhats thought that it was Buddha standing in front of them. Ananda was Buddha's cousin and looked like Buddha.

"No, it can't be Buddha," someone said. "It must be a buddha from some other world! Maybe it was due to our sincerity that some other buddha has arrived."

"No, it can't be a buddha from a different world," someone else said. "There is only Sakyamuni Buddha. There are no other buddhas from other worlds. It was Ananda who just walked past us, and it is he who is before us now. Could it be that Ananda has become a buddha too?"

Ananda knew that many people were questioning what had really happened. In order to clear up the confusion, he began each sutra with the phrase, "Thus have I heard," so that everyone would know that it wasn't Sakyamuni Buddha returning, nor was it another buddha from somewhere else, nor was it that Ananda had become a buddha. He was still Ananda. He had been present when Buddha was preaching, and now he was repeating what he had heard.

By saying "Thus have I heard," Ananda prevented misunderstanding in the minds of the audience. If the sutras had been Ananda's own, some disciples would have felt that since Ananda was on the same footing as they were, there was no reason to believe Ananda's speeches. When Ananda said "Thus have I heard," he meant "I have heard Buddha's teachings, and now I'm repeating them." There was nothing to argue about.

Today we can listen to and read the sutras because Ananda was able to tolerate complaints, be patient, and persevere through discipline. In this way, he developed the endurance which allowed him to attain arhathood, return to the assembly of monks and recite the sutras. Ananda had to undergo these tests, so shouldn't we expect the same endurance of ourselves? We must be constantly mindful and pattern ourselves after Ananda's patience and perseverance to realize our commitments to serve others.

Nanda's Lesson

Buddha was once walking past the royal palace. On the palace balcony, Nanda and his lovely concubine were leaning close together. When Nanda saw Buddha approaching, Buddha's gracefulness inspired a sense of respect. Without hesitation, Nanda came down from the palace and paid his respects to Buddha. Buddha handed his bowl to Nanda and said, "Come with me." Nanda then carried the bowl to the place where Buddha was staying.

"You shouldn't be infatuated with passion, because it's very dangerous," Buddha said to him. "You should renounce the world and become a monk. This is the only way to become truly free from suffering." Inspired by the tranquil atmosphere in the assembly of monks, Nanda chose to become a monk himself.

However, his mind was not tranquil and his desires constantly pulled him towards his palace and concubine. In the assembly, there were six monks who never followed the precepts. Nanda began to associate with them, and they constantly encouraged him to break the precepts.

One day, Buddha saw Nanda together with the six bad monks and called to him. Buddha took him to a busy market in a nearby village. In the market, there were many stalls selling meat and fish. On the ground were the leaves used for wrapping the meat and the fish, along with blood, fish scales and other dirty, discarded items.

Buddha told Nanda to pick up the leaves and smell them. Nanda picked up a handful of leaves and said, "Buddha, there is no need to bring them to my nose, because I can already tell they stink."

Buddha told him to throw the leaves away and to smell his own hands. "My hands are dirty and smelly," Nanda observed. Buddha instructed him to rub his hands with grass, but no matter how hard he tried, the smell was still there.

"You used to enjoy the luxury and the pleasure of passion in your palace," Buddha told him. "Now that you're a monk, you hang around with those six monks who never follow the precepts. Your personality is already as filthy as those dirty things on the ground. Although you aren't holding them now, your hands are still dirty. Even when you tried to rub your hands clean, the odor remained."

When Nanda heard this, he was quite embarrassed and wanted to apologize. Buddha then told Nanda to wash his hands. "From now on, these hands shouldn't touch anything dirty. Your mind has now been purified through your apology, and you should strive to keep it this way."

They continued walking through the village and passed an incense shop. Buddha told Nanda to go inside and get a box that had contained incense. Nanda went in and quickly brought a box back to Buddha.

"How does it smell?" Buddha asked him.

"It smells very fragrant," Nanda replied. "Now I know that there is a lot of expensive incense in the shop. Although it's just an empty box, it still smells wonderful."

"This is just like moral cultivation," Buddha responded. "Although the box is empty, it still has the sweet smell from the shop. The same logic applies to all the monks. You may not have had good training and you may not have comprehended the Truth and your own nature, but if you work and study alongside the older monks who have purified themselves, you can attain enlightenment very quickly. If you stay near Sariputra, Maudgalyayana or Mahakyasa, they can gradually help you elevate your character."

Buddha used this situation in ordinary life to teach Nanda a lesson and help him to realize his mistakes. He knew that Nanda was deeply infatuated with sensual pleasures and his mind was confused. So he educated Nanda with his wisdom and with the reality of life, allowing Nanda to comprehend the importance of spiritual training. Learning Buddhism is spiritual formation, and how do we cultivate the mind? Half of it comes from the strength of our friends, so being with people of high character is very important.

The Monk Brahmadatta

here was a monk named Brahmadatta in an assembly of more than 2,000 monks. After watching and learning from other monks for a long time, he was able to uphold the precepts but with one problem: he had a very bad memory. Other monks could understand the principles of Buddhism after listening to sermons. Brahmadatta seemed to understand the sermons while listening to them, but he completely forgot them after they were over.

Buddha told him to memorize verses, but after he had listened to them, he forgot them right away. Buddha then assigned 500 arhats to take turns teaching him. Three years later, Brahmadatta still couldn't memorize even a single verse, so many people considered him to be the most foolish monk of all. Buddha felt that everyone's wisdom was equal and that the difference was only in the method of instruction. To break through a student's obstacle, an instructor had to be patient and the student had to be attentive. Buddha was very compassionate with Brahmadatta, saying "You have to be patient and attentive while learning. Now you just need to memorize one verse." Buddha told Brahmadatta to look at him and concentrate entirely on him. Buddha told him to memorize this verse:

Guard your mouth and regulate your thoughts.
You shouldn't break the precepts.
Anyone who can do this can attain enlightenment.

Brahmadatta saw Buddha's compassionate face and heard his patient voice. He knew that he should appreciate Buddha's kindness, so he patiently kept on reciting. He finally memorized this verse and was able to repeat it fluently. Buddha was delighted and told him to recite it in front of everybody. Many people wondered whether he would remember this verse.

"You aren't young anymore, and it's nothing for you to just memorize one verse," Buddha said. "But the most important thing is to understand the essence of this verse. Don't say anything bad, don't be angry or greedy, and always act according to the precepts." When Brahmadatta heard this, he was suddenly able to understand everything in the world.

At that time, Buddha had assigned five hundred arhats to take turns instructing a group of nuns. One day, Buddha assigned Brahmadatta to teach them. When the nuns saw him coming, they started laughing. Since he couldn't even memorize one verse, why would Buddha appoint him to come here? They decided to make fun of him and embarrass him. They pretended to invite him to enter and sit at the podium. However, they sat arrogantly and treated him as a foolish old man.

Brahmadatta didn't care how they snubbed him. He sat down and began to speak. "I'm dull and don't learn much. The chants I remember are very few. If I make any mistakes, please let me know." Then he started to teach what Buddha had taught him about how to speak, think and act.

After listening to him, the nuns who had planned to argue with him couldn't open their mouths. The lesson was a big success. The nuns were very happy and they paid their most sincere respects to him.

Some people have so much wisdom that they're enlightened as soon as they hear a sermon, while others are so dull that they can't even memorize a rhymed verse. However, there is no absolute distinction between the two. From this story, we know that even a dull person will absorb the Buddhist teachings if he works hard and if the instructor is also attentive. In sum, whether it is teaching or learning, both sides must be patient and attentive. The way Buddha taught Brahmadatta was to make him understand how life and the human mind keep changing. If we can understand that thoughts and things come and go every second, then we will pay much more attention to the passage of time and work diligently for enlightenment and nirvana.

The Monk Sisi

Among Buddha's disciples was a monk named Sisi. He was a son of a sister of King Suddhodana, and so he was Buddha's cousin. After he became a monk, he still had the same bad habits he had acquired in the royal palace: arrogance and a sense of superiority. In the assembly, everyone respected former princes, and those former princes also respected other monks. Everyone, that is, except Sisi. When other people greeted him, he was very cold towards them because he despised them. Whenever others talked to him, he would just become angry and wouldn't treat them kindly. He always thought he was above everyone else and that others were simply worthless.

Buddha saw Sisi behaving with this condescending and arrogant attitude. One day, Buddha asked a young monk, "Are all of you friendly toward each other?"

The young monk replied, "Yes."

"Is there anyone in the assembly who is not cooperative?"

"Yes there is one. Sisi is arrogant, and yet he's lonely and unhappy because no one likes to talk to him."

"Tell him to come here."

The monk went and told Sisi that Buddha wanted to see him. When Sisi heard this, he didn't dare to be disobedient, and he went at once. Buddha asked him nicely, "Are you happy here?"

Sisi couldn't answer. He simply stared at the ground. He wasn't sure whether he was happy either.

Buddha asked again, "You're very unhappy, aren't you?"

Sisi lowered his head. Buddha told him, "Take a look at the monks behind you."

Sisi looked at the monks, who were talking happily with each other. He turned back and lowered his head again. "Buddha, I know I'm wrong. Because of my arrogance and hatred, I haven't been able to get along well with the other monks."

Buddha asked him, "Why can't you get along with the others? Think it over carefully."

Sisi pondered this silently and finally answered. "Buddha, I have a big ego and I look down on others. Whenever I see others being happy together, I just get angry, so I can't experience the joy of friendship. In short, my arrogance and contempt for others are too strong for me to be happy here."

Buddha reasoned with him. "Before you became a monk, you were a prince and also my cousin. Therefore you should set a good example by being humble. It's hard for you to be a monk when you still have your princely mentality. You must take advantage of this time for spiritual formation. You know that fame and wealth cannot last, so why are you so arrogant? If you want to be a good monk, you must overcome this attitude."

After Buddha had spoken, Sisi deeply repented. "I'll definitely correct my mistakes," he said. "I was wrong before, but from now on I'll study hard and approach others with wisdom and kindness."

Human beings must all live in this world, and in our daily lives we must learn to deal with other people, so we're happiest when everyone is friendly with each other. Learning Buddhism is learning to get along with other people. What kind of person is the easiest to get along with? It's the one with an open mind, lots of love, understanding, and forgiveness. A person who is narrow-minded and arrogant has a difficult time getting along with others.

If we want to learn to behave like Buddha and walk on the Path of the Bodhisattvas, we should start with a tranquil mind. If we're filled with arrogance or hatred, we ourselves will suffer in the end. We will simply isolate ourselves from others and will end up all alone, which is a miserable way to live. If we want to get along in this world, we must make other people happy and be accepted by them. Then, we will be able to preach the dharma to others.

The Slave Nafang

There was a small country called Nara, and the citizens there harvested pearls and sandalwood to support themselves. Although it was a small country, there were a lot of rich people, but there were also a lot of poor people.

At that time, there were two brothers whose parents had just died. The older brother wanted to divide the family property and work independently, so that neither one of them would burden the other. His wife asked, "How do we divide the property?"

Her husband didn't know how to do this fairly, so his wife made the decision. "One brother gets all the property, and the other gets the slave. That'll do." Of course the older brother received all the property, and his younger brother was assigned the slave.

The slave was an intelligent young man named Nafang. His parents had sold him to this family when he was a boy because they were too poor to raise him, but his old master had treated him very well and he was grateful. Now he was given to the younger brother, and he didn't know what he could give to his new master. More importantly, the young master had to look after him as an additional mouth to feed, so Nafang knew that he had to work tirelessly for him.

The young master, his family and Nafang left the house empty-handed. The master was quite worried because he had nothing in the world. Where could he live? How was the whole family going to live? "Master, you don't need to worry," Nafang comforted him. "Some-day I'm going to make you richer than your brother."

"How can that be?" his master replied. "I have nothing, and what are you going to use to earn money? We don't even have a place to live. How will I be richer than my brother?"

While they were pondering this, his wife suddenly remembered that she still had some necklaces and gold ornaments. She handed them to Nafang. "These are the only valuable items we have. Do something with them." Nafang took them to the market, thinking that he could buy something and sell it for a profit later. He couldn't find anything worth buying, so he left the city.

Just outside the city, he saw a man selling firewood. Among the firewood, Nafang discovered a piece of sandalwood. The sandalwood was good for curing illness, but the seller didn't know about its value. Nafang bought the firewood at a very cheap price and happily carried it back.

Not long afterwards, a very rich man became seriously sick. Although he had money, he couldn't find good sandalwood to mix with his medicine. When Nafang heard about this, he went to the rich man and gave him his piece of sandalwood. The rich man recovered and happily gave Nafang half of his property.

After Nafang received the money, he applied his financial skills, and a few years later his master was richer than his elder brother. Their life was stable and joyful, so one day the master asked his wife how they could repay Nafang. "The most valuable thing for a person is freedom," the wife said. "The most wonderful gift we can give Nafang is to set him free."

The master agreed, and spoke to Nafang. "You have given me so much, and I don't know how to repay you. So I have decided to give you half of my property and let you go free." When Nafang heard this, he was overjoyed and thanked his master for giving him back his freedom.

However, he told his master not to give him any money. "I only want freedom. I want to begin immediately to do spiritual formation. The reason that I'm poor in this life is that I lacked any moral cultivation in my previous life. Now I have my freedom, so I'm going to go to Buddha and ask him to accept me as his disciple. Therefore, I don't want any money."

Nafang went to Buddha and asked to be his disciple. Buddha was very happy and immediately accepted him as a monk. From then on, Nafang studied tirelessly. In a few years, he was quite familiar with Buddha's teachings and could recite them well.

Nafang strictly lived by the precepts and became one of the best at discussing Buddha's teachings. He was grateful to his former master for having given him back his freedom, and he wanted to repay him. So he asked Buddha for permission to leave the assembly and go back to his former master's home.

The master was delighted to see how dignified Nafang had become in religious life. He prepared many wonderful dishes, and they enjoyed the meal happily. After the feast, Nafang gladly shared with his former master the joy that he had received in learning the Buddhist teachings. The master was delighted to hear the

Buddhist dharma, and was anxious to hear Buddha himself speak.

"Buddha is very kind," Nafang said. "I can return and ask Buddha to come here to preach. This will also benefit the citizens of this country."

The master thought that that was an excellent suggestion. "That's wonderful! It isn't only I who should receive the joy of Buddha's dharma. I should report to the king and ask him to announce publicly that Buddha will come to our country. Then everyone will have a chance to hear his teachings."

When Nafang went back and made his request, Buddha compassionately agreed. The master also reported to the king and asked him to join the event. The king had heard about Buddha, so he was happy to participate, and he also made a public proclamation inviting all the citizens of his kingdom to come listen to Buddha preach. When Buddha and his disciples came, the king prepared a big banquet. When he saw Buddha, a wave of reverence welled up in his heart, and he sincerely prostrated himself before him.

After the feast, Buddha taught the crowds. During his sermon, the king and the master realized that the whole event had been made possible by Nafang. He was originally a slave. How could he have had the good fortune to become a monk and receive the dharma?

Buddha knew what they were thinking. "A person with a heart of gratitude knows to repay the kindness of others, and thus he has great fortune. Everyone should be grateful to each other. Because Nafang has a heart of gratitude, he has had good fortune and received much merit, and so has obtained enlightenment."

If everyone could be grateful to each other like Nafang, the slave who was grateful to his master, this could be a harmonious, perfect world. We must all learn that we must have gratitude in order to receive merit.

The Compassionate Prince Kunala

After Buddha passed away, there was a king named Usika. He was very kind and his government was very compassionate. He had a son with eyes as beautiful as the kunala, an Indian bird famous for its beautiful eyes. Because the king liked this kind of bird, he named his son Kunala. When Prince Kunala grew up, he was very handsome. His conduct was proper and he was very kind.

King Usika was a devoted Buddhist. One day, the king brought his son to a temple, and he asked a monk named Yasa about the Buddhist teachings. Yasa looked at the young prince. "Human life is impermanent," he said. "A body goes through the stages of birth, aging, illness and death, and human life is filled with impurity. Who can have the beauty of youth forever? All these are illusions. In the same way, although the prince's eyes seem beautiful, they are actually full of filth and the source of trouble."

The prince was quite puzzled. Everyone always praised him for his beautiful eyes, but why would the monk say that they were dirty and the source of trouble? These words kept whirling around in his head.

There were many concubines in the king's palace. One young lady was deeply attracted by Kunala's good looks. When she saw him sitting alone in the garden one day, she started to fondle him, trying to seduce him. But the prince was a righteous person and could not agree to such behavior. He pulled himself together and freed himself from her unwanted attentions.

Later, when the young prince was old enough to marry, King Usika found a wife for him. When the concubine saw the lover of her dreams married to someone else, she became intensely jealous and her love turned to hatred.

Not long after the marriage, the king became sick and the young concubine looked after him carefully until he recovered. He was grateful for her care and said to her, "Because you took care of me for such a long time, I will give you anything you desire."

She said, "I just want to rule the country for seven days."

The king thought to himself that since he had promised, he couldn't go back on his word. Besides, it was only for seven days. So he agreed.

When she was on the throne, the young lady wrote a letter filled with both love and hate and sent it to Prince Kunala. She wrote that her fury would only be placated if she never saw his eyes again. Now the prince finally realized what that monk had meant, but it was too late. The lady's word was like the king's command, and it couldn't be disobeyed.

Kunala reluctantly gouged out one eye and held it in his hand. "It's so disgusting," he suddenly realized. "Why would such a filthy little thing be praised by so many people and bring so much trouble? Since she wants both eyes, I'll take out the other one too." When both eyes were gone, everything before him was in total darkness, but his mind was suddenly filled with light. He felt the peace that comes from spiritual exaltation.

When his wife heard the news, she ran to the blind prince and started to wail with grief. But the prince was calm and consoled her with the Buddhist teachings. "Human life is brief, so don't harbor hatred or worry, because hatred and worry are your greatest enemies."

At that time, a bodyguard warned the prince, "Your Highness, I'm afraid that if you stay in the palace, your life will be in danger." The prince, of course, was already aware of this, and since he didn't want the court lady to continue making bad karma for herself by doing something even worse, he and his wife fled the palace. They learned to play the lute and to sing, and they wandered from town to town, making music in the streets. People would throw them a few coins, and in this way, the prince and his wife were able to feed themselves.

A few years later, they came back to the capital. One day, they wandered into the streets alongside the palace and started to sing. When King Usika heard the beautiful but mournful songs, he thought of his son, who had suddenly disappeared years before. He told his attendant to invite the musicians to enter the palace.

When the king saw the lute player, he realized that it was indeed the son that he had been thinking of day and night. When he saw how Prince Kunala had fallen from his royal life and was now only a blind lute-player singing on the streets for a living, the king was very upset. "Who did this to you?" he asked the prince. "Who made you lose your sight?" But Kunala refused to talk about it. He just told his father about the truths that he had learned, hoping his father would calm down.

At last, the ministers and the guards couldn't endure it any more and reported the truth to the king. He was furious and wanted to execute that concubine, but the prince begged his father to forgive her.

The king was touched by Kunala's compassion and released the young lady. However, in her own conscience, she was ashamed of herself and finally committed suicide. Because of her impure love, she had created trouble and hatred, hurt another person and destroyed herself. Was it all worth it?

If love could be pure and calm and nurture all creatures like clean water, it would be wonderful. I often say that we must guard our minds to bring the spirit of great love into full force. We must be careful not to let our minds become confused or filled with hatred. Above all, we must not let our minds become tainted with filthy desires.

Pindola Accepts an Invitation

Buddha had a disciple whose name was Pindola-bharadvaja. He was both clever and wise. He liked to show off his supernatural powers, acquired through meditation and deep concentration. To prevent such behavior, Buddha made a precept prohibiting his disciples from showing off their powers to attract the public.

Once, Pindola showed off again for a senior monk. When Buddha learned about it, he admonished him. "You intentionally exhibited your powers to impress people, so you may not enter nirvana. I'm punishing you by ordering you to preach the dharma until the end of time. If anyone sincerely invites you, you must appear before him to give witness to the dharma." After that, Pindola never entered nirvana.

About one hundred years later, Indian Buddhists all knew that Pindola had still not entered nirvana. They knew that if they prepared food for all the monks, that disciple would certainly appear.

At that time, when rich Indians built new houses or bathrooms, they always prepared meals for monks, hoping that Pindola would attend. Only rich families could build bathrooms. Most people, including monks, washed themselves when it rained or else they simply bathed in the rivers. So when rich families built their bathrooms, the first thing they did was hold a feast for the monks. And they always invited Pindola with the proper etiquette, as though a highly regarded monk was attending.

One day, a very rich man wanted to hold a big feast, so he spent a lot of money and decorated his house very lavishly. He invited Pindola and many monks, and he asked them to wear their finest robes. In order to show his respect and sincerity, he also set out many fresh flowers and a great deal of fruit. However, at the end of the day, the flowers had withered.

There was a tradition that if Pindola attended, the water would be clean and the flowers would be beautiful and fragrant and wouldn't wither. So, when the rich man saw the wilted flowers, he was unhappy. "I was very sincere," he thought. He asked a monk why Pindola hadn't come. The monk replied, "You weren't sincere enough!"

The man said, "Then I'll do it again."

The second time was also impressive. There were even more flowers and fruit than the last time. But again the flowers withered before the day ended. The man was very sad and asked many monks what went wrong. They all replied, "You still weren't sincere enough!" He said, "If that's so, then I'll use even more things and more impressive decorations to invite him!"

This time, the house was full of flowers and fruit, and hundreds of monks and guests were invited. The rich man very sincerely served food to each guest, one by one. When he had finished, he raised his head and saw that all the fruit and flowers were as fresh as ever. He happily thanked all the monks. However, he was quite puzzled, so he addressed all the monks. "I was also this sincere the first two times that I invited Pindola. I believe that he has arrived this time, but why didn't he come the first two times?"

A very old, well-dressed monk stood up. "You invited me three times," he said. "When I came the first time, your people guarded the door very tightly, and they allowed only the well-dressed monks to enter. My clothes were torn and ragged, so I couldn't go in. I told them that you had invited me. Not only wouldn't they let me in, they even beat me. When I was invited the second time, I also came, but I was beaten again. This time I put on new clothes and was allowed in."

The rich man finally realized that he had requested all the guests to dress up formally because he had wanted the place to be elegant and impressive, but instead he had bungled things up and prevented the most esteemed guest from entering.

Common people tend to have prejudices and forget their original sincerity. They make distinctions between rich and poor, young and old, high and low. We must always treat others equally.

Aniruddha's Past Causes

Aniruddha was one of Buddha's disciples. He was diligent in his moral cultivation, but he sometimes dozed off during the sermons. When Buddha admonished him for that one day, Aniruddha apologized and vowed not to fall asleep again. He never slept at all, and eventually he became blind.

One day when Aniruddha was mending his robe, he dropped his needle on the ground. Buddha picked it up for the blind monk and threaded it for him. From this simple action, everyone realized that Buddha cared very much about his disciples.

The disciples were really touched by Buddha's compassion, and they also wanted to know about Aniruddha's previous lives. "If you really want to know about his past, then I will tell you now," Buddha said.

At the time of Dipamkara Buddha [another buddha who lived hundreds of years before Sakyamuni Buddha], there was a young man who would go to the assembly to listen to the buddha's sermons. Dipamkara Buddha talked about the six magic powers. One of the powers was "super vision," which allows one to see every part of the universe, the past, the future, and the destiny of any creature. This young man was very interested in this super vision, and he vowed before the buddha that he would become the greatest expert with super vision in his future lives. After that, he started to work very hard to achieve this end.

After that life ended, the young disciple was reborn in a poor family. They were very poor and had nothing. He was tempted to steal, so one evening he put on his clothes and left the house. As he was passing a pagoda, the strap of his shoe suddenly broke, so he went into the pagoda. Someone had lighted a lamp in front of a statue. In order to see better so that he could fix the strap, the young man used a bamboo strip to raise the wick higher and added some oil to make the light brighter. After he fixed the strap, his mind was much calmer, as though that lamp had shone into his heart. He thought, "Even though I'm poor now, how can I think of becoming a thief? There are so many people around who are poor and starving. How can I rob them?" He felt that those thoughts of stealing were really dreadful. How could he want to do something that would only hurt others and yet wouldn't really help himself?

Standing in the pagoda, he repented and he vowed to begin his spiritual formation and to cultivate the power of super vision. He discovered that when he was confused and his mind was in darkness, he would easily make mistakes, so he hoped the lamp before him could enlighten his mind forever. Then his mind could develop super vision so that he could always see all matters clearly. He even vowed that in the future he would be born in a buddha's time, meet a buddha, and obtain the ultimate truth of life. From that moment on, no matter how bad things got, he never wanted to steal again.

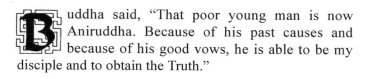 uddha said, "That poor young man is now Aniruddha. Because of his past causes and because of his good vows, he is able to be my disciple and to obtain the Truth."

Buddha taught Aniruddha to patiently train himself to open his heart, and he finally obtained the power of super vision. This was due to the causes that Aniruddha had planted in the past and the right conditions in Buddha's time for Aniruddha to obtain super vision. Buddha used this lesson to teach his disciples to spread their great love, to help each other, and to look after their minds.

When we are learning to behave like Buddha, we must remember: "Don't neglect to do any good deed, no matter how small it seems; don't do any evil deed, no matter how small it seems." Buddha hoped to teach his followers to be aware of their own speech and conduct in their daily lives and also to care for each other. We must remember that any little action now will have its effect later on. The seeds we plant in our current lives will bear fruit in this life and even in our future reincarnations.

Section 2
SAVING LIVES FROM THIS VULGAR WORLD

Religion isn't in a temple or a church but in each person's heart. We should spread the spirit of great love in all our daily behavior.

The Cause of Buddha's Difficulties

The Buddhist sutras tell us that after young Prince Siddhartha left the luxurious palace in which he had been raised and set off to find the path to the Truth, he encountered many difficulties that obstructed his spiritual development. For five years, he visited many different religious groups, but he wasn't satisfied with any of them. Next, he disciplined his body and mind as an ascetic for six years. During this time, the prince overcame many challenges, but there were also many demons which disrupted his study. Only after he abandoned asceticism did he attain enlightenment. Thus, the greatest difficulty that the prince encountered in his spiritual development was that it took him many years of study and practice before he arrived at the path to the Truth.

"Why did I take so long in spiritual formation and encounter so many difficulties?" Buddha once asked his disciples. "Demons also troubled me for a long time. Do you know why?"

"We don't know," his disciples replied. "Please tell us."

"Remember, I'm not the only buddha," Buddha pointed out. "I'm only one in a long line of buddhas who have come to this world to teach the truth and save all living beings. A story about an earlier buddha will help illustrate my point."

A t the time of Kyasa Buddha, there were two good friends. They grew up together and were very close to each other. They had similar interests, behavior and goals. One, named Husi, had heard that Kyasa Buddha had boundless blessings and wisdom and was now preaching to people. Husi was happy to hear about this, because he realized that Kyasa Buddha was an excellent teacher. He didn't want to miss this chance to learn from the buddha.

Husi didn't want his friend Homan to miss this chance to hear the buddha's teachings, so he went to Homan's home and said to him, "I have great news."

"What is it?" Homan asked.

"The great sage, Kyasa Buddha, has arrived in our city to preach. We must go and hear his teachings."

"What is there to see and hear? He's nothing but a bald monk!"

Husi saw that his friend wasn't interested, so he didn't go either. Three days went by. Husi heard many people praising the buddha's wisdom, so he went to Homan again. "Come on! We can't miss this chance!"

But Homan still had the same cynical attitude towards the buddha. "There's nothing good to listen to," he said. "He just talks about how to be a good person, and I already know that." Another three days passed by. Husi felt that if they kept on like this, both of them would miss this chance of a lifetime, so he went to Homan again.

Homan still had the same attitude, and Husi's temper finally flared up. He grabbed Homan's hair and said, "Whether you like it or not, you're coming with me!" Homan now realized his friend was serious and thought, "All right, maybe I should visit this sage."

"Don't get so upset," he told Husi. "Let go of my hair and I'll follow you."

So the two of them went to Kyasa Buddha, and Husi respectfully bowed before him. Seeing his friend's respectful attitude, Homan also bowed. Husi then faced Kyasa Buddha. "Buddha, my friend here doesn't know what your precious teaching is, and he doesn't cherish what he has. I ask you to instruct him, so that he can follow your teachings wholeheartedly." Kyasa Buddha praised them for coming and began preaching to transform Homan's mind.

Concluding his story, Sakyamuni Buddha explained its meaning. "Homan was my previous existence, and Husi was the heavenly being who helped me to escape from my father's palace. He guided me and helped my horse to fly over the castle walls.

"You can't let good opportunities slip by, and you must pay attention so that you don't make mistakes. In my incarnation as Homan, I was only reluctant for six days, but from that time on I have always had six years of obstacles in every life, including this one. I have had six years of hardship in this life. I spent six years going down the wrong path of ascetic practice. Therefore, everyone should constantly be careful to avoid my mistake."

Buddha had created these six years of obstacles in a previous lifetime, before he attained his buddhahood. We can take this story and apply it to ourselves. If our goal is correct at the start, we must persevere toward it. We have to appreciate the people and events around us, which allow us to develop ourselves spiritually. Our minds create our own obstacles and anxieties, and this is the most fearful. Not only must we try to eliminate these problems in our minds, but we also have to redeem ourselves and others from the suffering of the world.

The Monk on the Mountain

In Shinra (now in Korea), there was a young man from the royal household named Chin Chiao-chueh. He loved Buddhism and became a monk. Later, he thought that he could only learn Buddhism in China, so he caught a boat heading towards Anhui Province. When they were sailing near the Chinese coast, they encountered a storm that blew the boat to the shore and ran it aground. The young monk abandoned the boat and walked towards the mountains. Eventually, he came upon a beautiful plain. He decided to stay there for a while in a cave. He ended up living there for seventy-five years.

Chin's life was hard because he didn't have much food. He only ate wild grass and fruit, and it is even said that to stay alive, he ate dirt, which was called "Avalokitesvara dirt." [Avalokitesvara is also called Kuan Yin, the Goddess of Mercy.] We don't know if this was true or not, but certainly his life was very tough. There was no water near his cave, and he had to go half a mile down the mountain to get a bucket of water. Having to go up and down the mountain for water every day was very hard work.

A legend goes that one morning while Chin was meditating, he was suddenly bitten on the leg by an insect. He was surprised and came out of meditation. Then he saw a black-robed woman bowing before him. "I'm very sorry that my son so stupidly intruded on you," she said. "In order to show his true repentance and respect, he has changed himself into a stream of pure water at the cliff."

Then she disappeared. When he went to look, there was indeed a stream at the cliff not far from his cave. It is said that no matter how dry the weather was, the stream always flowed continuously.

The monk continued his spiritual formation for many years. One day, a group of poets, looking for ideas for poems, went there to enjoy the scenery. While strolling around, they suddenly saw a broken pot on a stone before a cave. The fire under the pot had gone out. In the pot, there were only wild plants mixed with Avalokitesvara dirt. When they looked inside the cave, they saw a monk deep in meditation, so everyone waited quietly for him at the mouth of the cave. It wasn't until the noon hour that the monk finally came out of the cave. The poets then asked him where he came from, because he didn't look Chinese. It is said that his appearance was very extraordinary: he was very tall and his forehead was rather wide. The monk said that he came from Shinra.

The poets were quite embarrassed, because they lived just at the foot of the mountain, but hadn't realized that a monk from so far away had been living on the mountain for so many years. The worst thing was that they had allowed him to live in such terrible conditions. They decided to become his supporters, and they also informed the lord of this mountain, Elder Min.

Min was a devout Buddhist. When he learned that there was an eminent monk living on the mountain, he was delighted. He went to visit him at once. When he saw that the monk lived in a cave, he felt very sorry and, with the help of the poets, built a simple house for him.

Min had also wanted to offer food to one hundred monks every day, but strangely, no matter what he did, there were always ninety-nine monks. He invited Chin to make a total of one hundred, and the old monk often went to Min's home to receive these meals.

When Chin had been provided with everything he needed, he was able to study much harder. His supporters turned to him to learn the Buddhist teachings. Min respected Chin very much, so he allowed his son to train as a monk with him.

One day, the lord of the mountain talked to the old monk about enlarging his house. "More and more devotees are coming to see you. In the future, others will live and study here too. Do you want to enlarge your house?"

"If there's enough space, then I will do it."

"The whole mountain is mine, so you can have as much space as you want."

"All I need is an area about as big as my robe."

"That isn't big enough!" Min retorted.

"The ground covered by the shadow of this robe will be sufficient."

The elder agreed, so Chin took off his robe and threw it into the air. It was like a dark cloud blocking the sun and turning the whole mountain black, as though the mountain was covered by the robe. The elder was overwhelmed, and he happily presented the whole mountain to the monk. His friends the poets then began to consider what to call the mountain. Because the mountain looked like the nine petals of the lotus flower, it was named Chiuhua ("nine flower").

More devotees gradually came and the temple
expanded successfully. The monk helped many people,
and many Korean monks also came to live and study
there. The number of monks increased year after year.
Because there were so many monks, there was once a
shortage of food. Chin encouraged some monks to go
elsewhere, but everyone enjoyed living there, and
although their lives were difficult, they still wanted to follow Chin. No one was willing to leave the mountain.

Chin was called a transformation of Ksitigarbha Bodhisattva. Ksitigarbha is also known as the Great Vow
Bodhisattva, because he vowed not to be enlightened
until he had redeemed all living beings from the suffering
of the world. Even now, he still preaches the Buddhist
dharma in hell to rescue souls from their punishment.

Why was Chin thought to be Ksitigarbha? In the daytime he would preach to the public, but in the evening he
would meditate. It is said that at night on the mountain,
people could hear the sounds of the tools of torture used
in the hells. The rumor started that Chin preached in the
hells every night, just like Ksitigarbha.

A Rich Young Man Repents

There was a young man who was the only child of a rich old couple. His parents spoiled him completely, and as a result the young man had no manners and indulged in alcohol. His parents tried to convince him to change his ways, but he wouldn't listen.

The old man thought his son behaved this way because he hadn't been given any responsibility. Without any duties or obligations, the young man just wasted his time. The old man thought that giving his son the family business might provide him with a sense of responsibility and that his son would then change his ways.

However, after the young man took over the business, he only became worse. Whenever he went out, he would be gone for seven or eight days. He had a group of hooligan friends with whom he wasted his time enjoying wine, women and song. Within a few years, his wealth was gone and he had to beg to stay alive. His friends were nowhere to be seen, and even when they saw him on the streets, they didn't want to help him. Some people gave him money, but when they realized who he was, they took the money back. People who had been swindled by him in the past would chase him down and beat him.

Tired of such a desperate life, the young man returned home, hoping that his parents would still welcome him. He thought that at least at home he would be warm and he would have three meals a day. But his parents had long since grown tired of his behavior and wouldn't let him in the door.

H e had heard that the most compassionate person in the world was Buddha, who had an open mind and would take anyone in. The young man thought that he might as well go to Buddha and become his disciple. Then he wouldn't need to worry about meals anymore and wouldn't be beaten up either. So he went to the place where Buddha was staying.

Buddha saw him and asked, "What do you have in mind?"

"I have no place to go and no food to eat," the young man said. "I hope that with your compassion you will take me in."

"The most compassionate, the most caring, and the most forgiving persons in the world are your parents," Buddha said. "If you can change your ways, they will certainly forgive you. If your mind is filthy, you will always be filthy even if you're a monk. The most important thing right now is to cleanse your mind. While your parents are still alive, go home now, ask for forgiveness and work to make them happy. If you can work hard, treat your parents respectfully, choose your friends carefully, and do things honestly, you can certainly start your life anew."

Buddha taught him patiently, and the young man went home. No matter how his parents wanted to throw him out, he knew that no one would care more about him than his parents. He now knew why his parents had been angry at his mistakes, but he also knew that his parents would forgive him. He knelt before them and earnestly asked their forgiveness.

His parents felt that if they were too severe, he might actually leave and never come back. However, they had to show their anger and disappointment. This is the mentality of all parents. But when they saw him repenting so earnestly, they finally said, "If you really want to start again, we can forgive you."

"Only a father really knows his son." The old man hadn't given all his money to his son, so he still had some left. Now his son had changed, so he gave the rest to him to help him establish his new life.

Indeed, the young man was truly transformed and he started over from the beginning. He worked very hard, spoke truthfully, respected his parents, and was polite and sincere to other people. With such exemplary behavior, he even received the praise of his relatives. Within three years, he became a successful, respected citizen and a filial son.

A person needs to be disciplined in order to know the true source of hardship. Discipline can help us to change.

The Monk From Snow Mountain

There was a Buddhist follower whose family was falling apart due to his extramarital affair. His wife couldn't take it anymore and even thought of committing suicide. Buddha told the man a story to save his family.

There was a monk who lived on Snow Mountain. One day he got dressed, packed up his things and went down the mountain to buy oil, salt and rice. He was full of good spirits in the morning air, and he walked with a dignified air. When he arrived at the city gate, the king saw the monk and sensed his nobility. The king greeted him and invited him to the palace, where he prepared a sumptuous feast for him.

The king enjoyed watching the monk's proper conduct, so when the monk finished his meal, the king asked him to talk about the Buddhist teachings. The monk spoke eloquently and taught the king all that he had learned. The king was filled with the joy of the dharma. "Please don't go back. I hope you will stay in the palace so that you can constantly preach to me and allow me to understand this other-worldly philosophy." The monk was also happy, because he thought that it would be good for him to stay in the palace and teach the dharma, so he agreed to the king's request. The monk stayed for sixteen years. Both the king and the monk got along well with each other and learned a lot from each other.

One day, enemies attacked the border of the country, so the king led his armies out to defend it. Before he left, he ordered a lady of the court to provide meals for the monk. One day, when she had prepared lunch, the monk hadn't yet arrived. She was very tired and took a bath. She then put on a light dress and lay down to take a nap.

Just then, she heard footsteps approaching, and she knew it was the monk coming for his lunch. She rushed to get out of bed just as the monk arrived at the door. In her hurry, she accidentally dropped her dress. At that instant, the monk saw her. He couldn't take his eyes off her tender body. The lady was embarrassed and put on her dress at once. She then invited him to enter for his lunch. Although there were piles of delicious food, the monk was absent-minded and didn't enjoy the meal. After lunch, he went back to his room for a nap, but he was too restless to sleep. He couldn't eat for seven days, he couldn't sleep for seven days, and he was sick for seven days.

The king then returned from his victory. Before entering his palace, he went around and inspected the city. When he came to the monk's lodging just outside the palace, he decided to stop in for a visit. He found that the place was a filthy mess, and he saw the monk lying on his bed, apparently sick. The king ordered his soldiers to clean up the place. Then he sat on the edge of the bed and asked the monk if he was sick.

"Your Majesty," the monk replied, "I'm not sick, but my mind is in turmoil."

"Why is that?" the king asked.

He replied honestly, "I saw the lady's body and lost my composure."

The king then said, "If you want her, then I will give her to you. Get up and come with me."

The monk put on his clothes and went with the king to the main hall. The king requested the court lady to present herself. The king told her, "From now on, you will live with the monk."

Later, when the monk wasn't around, the king told her secretly, "He's sick because of you, so try to help him."

"I understand," she answered, "and you can count on me." So she followed the monk out of the palace.

"Where are you taking me?" she asked him. "We should have a house."

He thought for a while and then asked, "Where can I get a house?"

"Why don't you ask the king for one?"

So he went back to the king, and the king indeed gave him a house in the city. It was a building where piles of junk were stored. The monk brought the lady there, and she took one look. "Look, the house is full of garbage and it needs to be cleaned up. First I want you to sweep the floor, and then I want you to wipe the walls clean."

"Where should I start?" he asked.

"Go to the palace and get a broom, a dustpan, and other cleaning supplies. Then get back here and sweep out this house."

So the monk went back to the palace and got the supplies. He then gave the house a thorough cleaning. When he finished, he was dirty and sweating, but the lady wasn't satisfied. "Now the house is empty, so you need to move some furniture here. We need a table, chairs, a bed..."

He meekly went back to the palace and asked for some furniture. He carried the things one by one to the house and set them up. Then she said, "I want to take a bath now, so hurry up and get some soap and towels and fill the tub with water." He did as she demanded. After she finished her bath, he finally took a bath too.

Afterwards, the monk sat on the bed. Suddenly, the lady grabbed the monk's beard and pulled his face close to hers. "You've forgotten that you're a monk. Now that we're so close to each other, why don't you take a good look at my face!"

He was stunned at this unexpected reaction. With her face pressed against his, all he could see was a white blur. Furthermore, he was exhausted from the day's work. At that moment he suddenly realized that a woman's beauty was really harmful! He had toiled hard all day long, and what had he gotten for it? Nothing but a white blur! His impure lust had destroyed his contemplation and filled his heart with confusion, and all for a pretty woman.

Thus enlightened, he pushed himself away from her. "I've come to my senses and I'm sending you back to the king. I'm going back to Snow Mountain to spend my days in spiritual formation and to enjoy the tranquillity of meditation." He sent her back to the palace immediately, and without another thought for life in the palace, he returned to Snow Mountain.

When Buddha finished the story, he admonished the adulterous follower. "Even this monk lost his self-control just because of his desire for a woman. It is no wonder that since you're only a layperson living in this vulgar world, you can't avoid having the same desire. But you have to be aware of your thinking at all times. When you sense that you're thinking about women other than your wife, you must get hold of your-self immediately and go look after your wife and your family. You must take on a husband's responsibility and build a beautiful family."

This is a story that Buddha told to a lay follower, and it was also a lesson in the reality of life. From their desires, humans plant the seeds of suffering and receive the results later. Buddha said that sexual desire was the most dreadful thing, because not only laypeople could be confused by desire, but even disciples who had attained the highest level of contemplation and supernatural pow-ers could become lost before a beautiful woman. Most problems in families and society arise from this desire. So if we want to learn Buddhism, we must control our thoughts at all times.

The Prince and the Monk

ne day, Buddha saw some of his disciples sitting together and talking, so he went and sat with them. A disciple asked Buddha, "Why is it that some people are always grateful to others, and other people aren't? I feel sorry for those who aren't."

Buddha asked him, "Can you give an example?"

"Well, there's your cousin Devadatta," he replied. "He was your cousin before he became a monk, and then he was your disciple. But why does he continuously try to hurt you and destroy the order of monks? Isn't his life bitter?"

"Yes, I feel sorry for him too," Buddha said. "His mind is full of hatred and perplexity. Other people dislike him too, so he's unhappy and has this hatred against many people."

"We don't understand this," the disciple observed. "He has accepted your teachings and understands the foundation of Buddhism. He ought to be grateful. But why can't he be so?"

"He has accumulated these bad habits for a long time. He didn't become like this in this generation. He has been ungrateful for eons. You will understand why after I tell you about one of Devadatta's previous lives."

long time ago, there was a jealous prince who always treated others with hatred, and he was mean to the servants in the palace too. No matter how kind other people were to him, he never felt grate-

ful, nor did he feel any compassion towards other people. As he grew older, his jealousy, hatred and hostility
became stronger. No one in the palace was happy with
him, but no one dared to say anything about it either.
Even the ministers knew that the prince was a very hostile person.

One day he decided to swim in a lake. It was already
dark and a storm was coming. The wind and the rain grew
stronger, and people warned the prince against going, but
he didn't care. He still insisted on going swimming, so he
and his attendants went to the lake. When they arrived, his
attendants, who had been bullied by the prince for a long
time, already had a plan. As the wind howled, the rain fell
in sheets, and the thunder boomed, they suddenly pushed
the prince into the lake and then ran back to the palace.

A minister saw them and asked, "How come you're
back? And where is the prince?"

"We became separated in the bad weather," the attendants answered. "Hasn't the prince returned yet?" The
minister thought that the prince could be in danger, so he
reported it to the king. The king immediately ordered
everyone out to look for the prince. They searched for
him everywhere, but they couldn't find him.

Meanwhile, the prince struggled in the water where
he had been thrown. He touched a log and clam-
bered onto it. A snake, a mouse and a parrot were
on the log too. They floated on the lake in the heavy rain
and howling wind. The prince cried out with fear, and his
shouting was very sad and sorrowful.

A monk lived in a tent by the lake. He heard the cries
and saw the bad weather. It was very dark, and he felt that

that person's life must be in great danger in weather like this. He ran to the lake and saw the prince on the log. Without a thought for his own safety, he jumped into the lake, swam out to the log, and pushed it to the shore. He first pulled the prince from the log. When he saw the snake, the mouse and the bird, he carefully picked them up and took them to his tent.

The monk lit a fire and treated the snake's injuries first. He then examined the mouse and the bird before he finally treated the prince. The monk also prepared some food. He let the bird, the mouse and the snake eat first, and then he brought a share to the prince. But the prince didn't appreciate his help and was quite angry. He felt that since the monk didn't examine or feed him first, he showed disrespect for his royal rank.

The animals recovered the next day, and the monk told them, "You have all recovered, so you may return."

"I will never forget your compassion," said the snake to the monk. "If you run into any difficulty anywhere, just call 'Snake! Snake!' and I'll come help you."

"I'm also grateful for your kindness and I will repay you," the mouse said. "If you need me, just shout, 'Mouse! Mouse!' and I'll come to you."

The bird said, "No matter where you might be, if you need me, just yell, 'Parrot! Parrot!' and I'll come to you."

The prince also mouthed false words of gratitude. "Thank you very much for saving my life. After I become the king, I will repay you if you come to see me." Actually, the prince wanted revenge against the monk. He went home, and not long afterwards he became the new king.

ne day, the monk wanted to know whether there was any difference between a human's mind and an animal's mind, so he went to the city to attend the prince's coronation ceremony. On the way, he wondered whether the snake would appear as it had said, so he called, "Snake! Snake!" The snake appeared as he had promised. "I'm very happy to see you. Because you're my savior, I want to tell you that in my past life I hid some gold bars underground. Because of my greed, I was reborn as a snake to guard over that gold. If I give it to you, I will be free from this form."

The monk said, "Since you think this way, then just keep it for me." He thanked the snake and hoped that it would be free soon.

After walking a little further, he wondered about the mouse too, so he shouted, "Mouse! Mouse!" The mouse also appeared as he had promised. "I used to be a good friend of the snake in our previous life. We both wanted to make money and keep it all for ourselves. But life is short and I soon died. In order to guard this money, I was reborn as a mouse. I'm in agony in this life. I hope you can accept this money and I will be free." The monk replied, "Just leave it there and I'll use it later." The monk also thanked the mouse.

After a while, he thought about the bird, so he yelled, "Parrot! Parrot!" The parrot happily appeared before the monk and said, "My savior, if you need me, I can call upon a huge flock of birds to collect rice seeds to repay your kindness."

"I'm very grateful that you have this kind of strength," the monk answered. "When I need you, I'll call you. I hope your strength will be able to support me."

He continued walking into the city and ran into the new king parading down the street after the coronation ceremony. The king saw him and whispered to his guards. "See that old guy? He's a very strange person, so don't let him come near me. I want you to arrest him, beat him up, and then throw him out of the city. Don't let him see me." The guards went to the monk and started beating him. The monk ran for his life while the guards chased him and beat him all the way out of the city. As the monk was being beaten, he cried, "The old sages used to say, 'Humans and animals have the same mind,' but the man I saved wants me dead!"

The guards heard these words and wondered what they meant, so one of them stopped the others and asked the monk what he had meant. After finding out the truth, the guards returned to the city and announced it to the crowd: the most respectable person was the monk, because he had saved the new king's life, while the most detestable person was the new king, because he hadn't shown any gratitude to the monk and had ordered him beaten! All the people were shocked and disgusted by the king's evil mind.

The crowd dragged the king from his horse and threw him out of the city, forbidding him to ever enter the city again. They also carried the monk back to the city and treated his injuries. When he had recovered, they put him on the throne. The citizens loved the monk because of his compassion.

One day, the monk recalled the words of the snake and the mouse, so he told his people where they could find the money and told them to dig it up. Then he gave the money to all the poor people in the country.

"Devadatta was that prince and I was the monk," Buddha said. "After many generations, Devadatta's hatred is still there."

Buddhism teaches that the mind is always changing. Ideas and thoughts constantly arise and disappear in the mind. In one minute, the mind is filled with the joy of life, but in the next minute, there's hatred or sadness. In this story, the prince first felt gratitude towards the monk when he was rescued, but later on he only remembered that the monk didn't treat his wounds or give him food first, so the prince became angry and hated the monk. He totally forgot that he owed him his life. This is how a mind changes. So we have to be constantly aware of our minds.

The Jealous King and the Elephant

During Buddha's time, every disciple respected Buddha very much, except one—Devadatta. Although he was a monk, he was jealous of Buddha. He constantly tried to spread disharmony and ill-will among the community of monks. He even slandered Buddha's speech and conduct. If he heard people praising Buddha, he would try to alienate them by spreading rumors.

One day, some monks were discussing Devadatta's behavior. "Why is Devadatta always so dissatisfied with Buddha? Why does he keep spreading so many rumors?"

Buddha passed by and asked, "What are you talking about?"

"Buddha, we're very confused," one disciple replied. "Devadatta is your cousin and he's also your disciple. Why is he always obstructing you? Why is he always slandering you and lying about you? What kind of karmic relationship did you and Devadatta make in the past?"

"Devadatta hasn't just slandered me in this generation," Buddha replied. "He has been jealous of me for many generations, and he has often attempted to injure me. Have a seat, and I'll tell you a story from one of his past lives."

There was once a country called Mocita. The king had an elephant whose fine skin was pure white. It was very intelligent, and everyone who saw it praised it for its grace and beauty.

One day, there was a big religious festival. The king rode this elephant among the crowd to inspect the groups arriving for the ceremony. When the white elephant appeared, everyone was very pleased and praised it, because it was so beautiful and its movements were so elegant and firm.

When the king saw the people praising the white elephant instead of his own shining, heroic figure, he became very jealous and angry. He wanted the elephant dead.

The king asked the trainer, "Is the elephant well trained?"

"Yes, Your Majesty," the trainer said. "It is very intelligent and easy to train."

"If it stands on the highest cliff, can it perform the skills that it's been taught?"

"No problem."

The king said, "All right, I want to see this white elephant perform."

So the king ordered the elephant to perform on a dangerous cliff on the highest mountain in Mocita. The trainer led the elephant to the cliff, where the king and a crowd of officials and people were waiting for the elephant to perform. The king wanted the trainer to ride on top of the elephant to give it its orders. The king commanded, "I want you to make it stand on three legs." So the trainer ordered the elephant to stand on three legs. The elephant did so very gracefully, and the crowd applauded. When the king saw this, he became even angrier and said, "Now I want it to stand on two legs." The elephant did so, and the ooh's and ah's from the crowd became even louder. The king was more jealous than ever, so he commanded the elephant to stand on one leg. He didn't think the elephant could do it. But when it really stood on one leg at the edge of that dangerous cliff, the applause was like thunder.

Now the king was furious. He gnashed his teeth and insanely screamed, "Now I want it to lift all four legs and hover in the air!"

At this, the trainer leaned down and whispered into the elephant's ear. "The king wants you dead. Such an irrational king doesn't deserve your services. Can you fly to the country of Polona?" The elephant nodded and floated lightly into the air with the trainer on its back. It flew across the cliff and on to Polona.

In Polona, people looked up and saw a white elephant floating in the air with a man riding on its back. They shouted with amazement. "Wow! What an amazing white elephant! He's bringing good fortune to Polona and this is a good sign!" The citizens knelt on the ground and shouted with joy. The king heard the news, and he and his ministers ran out from the palace to see it. He said, "I wonder if it will come down here."

The elephant indeed landed next to the palace. The king asked the trainer, "Where are you from?"

"Your Majesty, we are from Mocita."

"This elephant will certainly bring good fortune to my country. I hope it can stay."

The trainer turned and spoke to the elephant. "This is a good, caring king. We should stay here and serve him." So they stayed. The king was very happy and gave the elephant the title of Elephant King. He also built a good house for him and fed him with excellent food.

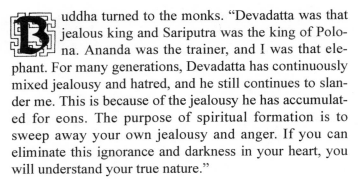

uddha turned to the monks. "Devadatta was that jealous king and Sariputra was the king of Polo-na. Ananda was the trainer, and I was that elephant. For many generations, Devadatta has continuously mixed jealousy and hatred, and he still continues to slander me. This is because of the jealousy he has accumulated for eons. The purpose of spiritual formation is to sweep away your own jealousy and anger. If you can eliminate this ignorance and darkness in your heart, you will understand your true nature."

There's nothing special in learning Buddhism. The most important thing is to look after your mind.

Mika Slanders Dravya

Buddha and his monks always went from door to door to beg for food. The main purpose of this was to rid the monks of their egoism. Buddha appointed his disciple Dravya, who was righteous and had a good spiritual formation, to be in charge of assigning the routes for each of the monks. He arranged for every monk to go in a certain direction and ask certain families for food every day. Every three days, everyone changed routes.

There was a young monk named Mika. He hadn't been a monk very long, so he still had the same habits as ordinary people. Once he was assigned to a certain village. The people there weren't rich and gave him very plain, simple food. When he saw this, he was very unhappy, but he still had to eat it. The food on the second day was worse, and the food on the third day was awful. He grumbled and became angry with Dravya, because he thought Dravya had intentionally assigned him to that village.

His sister, Mitra, was a nun. One day, Mika went to talk to her and vent his anger. She was too young to judge right from wrong, so she believed every word he said. She was indignant at the injustice that he had suffered. When he saw her reaction, his anger became even worse.

He told her, "You have to help me!"

"I'll help you any way I can."

"There's only one way. You must go to Buddha and tell him that Dravya broke the precepts by sexually harassing you."

Mitra was shocked. "I can't do that! He strictly abides by the precepts and you want me to slander him! I can't do it!"

"If you don't want to, then you can forget that I'm your brother. I don't have a sister like you!" Mitra was in a dilemma, but she finally agreed.

They went to Buddha and bowed before him. Mitra said, "Buddha, there's a monk who has broken the precepts!"

Buddha asked, "Who?"

"It is Dravya," she said.

Mika said, "Buddha, it's true."

Buddha saw Dravya nearby, so he called him. "You heard this young nun's word. Is it true?"

Dravya replied, "Buddha should know whether it is true!"

"This is not the answer I want," Buddha said. "If it's true, then say yes. If it isn't true, then say no."

Another disciple, Rahula, stood up. "Dravya has broken the precepts, and Mika and Mitra are both here to accuse him. If Dravya simply says that he didn't do it, will he be considered innocent?"

Buddha turned to him. "Rahula, if Mika came to me and said, 'Rahula has broken the precepts!' and Mitra came to affirm it, what would you say?"

"If I didn't do it, then of course I would answer no. Buddha should know that."

"Then isn't your answer the same as Dravya's? Young people should logically analyze everything in detail." Buddha then turned to the other monks. "I want you to look into this matter. I want Mitra to go outside so all of you can question Mika." Then Buddha left.

The monks then began questioning Mika. "When did you see Dravya molesting your sister? Was there anyone else around? Or were you the only one that saw it?"

The monks kept asking Mika, and there were many questions that he didn't know how to answer. He realized that he had made a mistake and felt ashamed. He then admitted that he had intentionally made up the story to slander Dravya and that Mitra had accused him because he had told her to. This all happened because he had been assigned to a poor village where the food was bad.

The truth came out and Buddha returned. The monks reported their findings to Buddha and Dravya was declared innocent.

ika was very embarrassed and sincerely apologized to Buddha for his actions. Buddha admonished him. "If you don't look after your mind, anger, greed and delusion can easily arise. It is greed to seek delicious food! Since you have become a monk, you should only think of food as something to nourish the body, nothing more. But you clung to your taste for fine food, so your anger appeared when you considered that food bad. You then turned your anger on the monk who serves the assembly. You even deceived your sister into making a false accusation. All this happened because of the three poisons of anger, greed and delusion in your mind."

Mika wished that there were a hole in the ground that he could hide in. He was determined to correct his mistakes and to study diligently.

The assembly of monks was pure and righteous, but events like this were unavoidable. It isn't surprising that even in our own time our minds are mostly governed by the things around us. Anger, greed and delusion often appear in our daily behavior. We must learn Buddha's tranquil mind and behavior so that we can be as pure as a flowing mountain stream.

A Man Named "Unfortunate"

Since ancient times, especially among some races in the Far East, the notion has been implanted in people's minds that changing one's name can alter one's fate. When a baby is born, his parents call in a fortune-teller to give him a lucky name.

In Buddha's time, there was a young man named Anathapindika, who was very, very rich. Kings and princes respected him, and farmers, shopkeepers, and other people honored him too.

Anathapindika had a good friend who had grown up in poverty. He was called "Unfortunate." The rich young man saw that this friend was destitute, so he hired him as a servant. But Anathapindika's family members and friends didn't like him very much, because they had to say, "Unfortunate, come!" "Unfortunate, sit!" "Unfortunate, eat!" It always made them feel like they were asking some unfortunate bad fate to arrive.

They said to Anathapindika, "You should fire him and throw him out."

Anathapindika couldn't understand this. "He's a nice person, so why should I do that?"

"Because his name is Unfortunate," they said. "When we say, see, and hear 'Unfortunate' every day, we're afraid it will be 'unfortunate' for us."

"You're wrong," Anathapindika replied. "Buddha once said that a person's fate comes from his karma, which is the results of his past actions. Whether that person is fortunate or not depends entirely on his past actions. If that person has good karma, he will have good fortune. If he has bad karma, he will have bad fortune. If he has good fortune and his name is 'Unfortunate,' he will still be a fortunate person. If he has no fortune but his name is 'Wise,' he will be neither wise nor fortunate. So we shouldn't be superstitious about a name. We should look at a person's past causes and the current environment that will help to bring out the results of those past actions!" Anathapindika was a follower of Buddha, and he understood concepts like "karma" and "past causes" and "fortune." Since he had said this, the other people had nothing else to say.

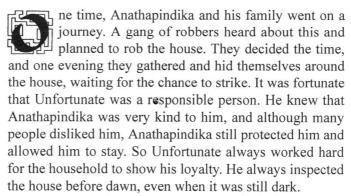 ne time, Anathapindika and his family went on a journey. A gang of robbers heard about this and planned to rob the house. They decided the time, and one evening they gathered and hid themselves around the house, waiting for the chance to strike. It was fortunate that Unfortunate was a responsible person. He knew that Anathapindika was very kind to him, and although many people disliked him, Anathapindika still protected him and allowed him to stay. So Unfortunate always worked hard for the household to show his loyalty. He always inspected the house before dawn, even when it was still dark.

That morning while he was inspecting outside the house, he discovered that there were strange people around who were acting very suspiciously. So he went around and told other people to get their drums and gongs and to start beating them. The racket scared off the robbers. They ran away, leaving their weapons behind on the ground.

The next day, Anathapindika's servants came out and were astonished to see all sorts of weapons scattered on the ground. If the robbers had been successful, all the household treasures would have been taken. When Anathapindika returned, they reported the whole affair to him and praised Unfortunate. "Unfortunate is a wise man. If it hadn't been for his watchfulness, the household would have suffered serious loss."

Anathapindika was very delighted and thanked Unfortunate for all he had done. He told the story to Buddha, who then praised Anathapindika. "This happened because you were wise enough to persuade your family and friends to allow such a good person to stay at your place. If you had been as superstitious as them, you wouldn't have escaped this misfortune. You know the logic of cause and effect, and you don't judge another person because of his name. Therefore, you are very fortunate."

Some people consider their own fates bad and grumble when they encounter just one little problem. Then they look for shamans or soothsayers to help them change their fates. This is simply incorrect. Actually, the most important thing is to know what kind of seeds we planted in the past—our good and bad actions in our previous lives—so we will know what kind of path we will walk on in this life. Our names have nothing to do with our fates. It is our behavior that makes the difference. What we do now will create results in our next reincarnations. If we can manage our speech and conduct now, we will receive good fortune in the future. In sum, the seeds from our past lives bear their fruits in this life. If we create more good fortune and cultivate our wisdom, we can eliminate disasters and turn bad into good.

Jetavana Garden

Anathapindika hoped that Buddha would come to Sravasti to teach and help the public, so he spent a lot of money to buy a piece of land from Prince Jeta. He even covered the ground in the garden with gold. While he was doing all this, the members of another religious cult heard the news and were shocked. They felt that the city was their turf. If Buddha came, their teachings would be greatly affected and fewer people would make offerings to them. So they thought about ways to interrupt the construction.

The first thing they did was to go to Anathapindika and protest his plans. "Why should that Gautama come here? He already has a place to stay, so why are you inviting him here? What power does he have?" They kept harassing Anathapindika, but they couldn't make him change his mind.

Seeing that their protest was useless, they went to the king. The king had heard of Buddha and liked his teachings, so he didn't pay any attention to them either. Then, they went back to Anathapindika and said, "If you really want to invite Gautama's assembly here, he has to meet one condition, or we won't give up."

"What is it?" Anathapindika asked. "If everyone can live in peace, I'll try to meet your condition."

"Gautama has a wise disciple named Sariputra, and we want him to compete against us."

Anathapindika didn't think that was difficult, so he went to Rajagrha and reported that cult's demand to

Buddha. Buddha felt that this was a good chance to introduce his teachings in Sravasti, so he told Sariputra to go there. "The construction of the garden is under way. You'd better go first to pacify the cult there, so that they won't make any more trouble for us." Sariputra happily agreed.

Anathapindika asked Sariputra, "When will you be ready to compete against them?"

"In seven days," he replied. "I'll give them seven days to prepare." Anathapindika went back to Sravasti and told the religious cult there to get ready.

Among the cult members, there was one highly respected leader, who felt that this competition would be crucial for them. If they lost, Gautama would be allowed to come in, and their benefits and social status would be greatly affected. Therefore, they had to be very careful. During the seven-day period, they rounded up the best people they could find, and they invited many others to be present that day for support. Anathapindika was also serious about this event. He set up a stage and arranged the seats for both sides.

When the day came, a vast number of cult members arrived, but Sariputra came alone. "All right, the time has come," Sariputra said. "Do you want to compete with a philosophical debate or with supernatural powers?"

"It will be faster to compete with supernatural powers," they replied.

The cult leader transformed himself into a very beautiful garden with flowers blooming and their sweet scent everywhere. Sariputra changed himself into a gentle breeze. The flowers swayed in the wind, and the leaves and petals fell off. The cult lost this first round.

Then the cult leader changed himself into a pond of water that was so clear that one could see the bottom of the pond. Sariputra changed himself into an elephant and took a bath in the pond. When the elephant turned himself over in the pond, the water became muddy. They lost again.

The leader was quite angry, so he changed himself into a vicious nine-headed dragon and hurtled towards Sariputra. Sariputra then changed himself into a gigantic golden-winged roc. It flew up with ease and sat firmly on the dragon's head. No matter how the dragon turned and twisted, it couldn't shake the huge bird off. At this, the cult members were awestruck and conceded defeat. Some of them immediately asked to join the Buddhists, but some stubborn diehards were still not convinced and left.

These stubborn followers still wanted to stop the construction of the garden, so they pretended to be laborers and asked Anathapindika for work. Anathapindika knew what they were up to. He reported to Sariputra, who then said, "If we want the construction to go faster, we certainly need to hire more workers. All right, we'll allow them to come." Sariputra personally inspected the construction.

One day, a group of these workers came at Anathapindika with clubs, shovels, and other tools. Suddenly, the workers started to feel fatigued and sleepy. No matter how hard they tried to walk, their legs became too sluggish to move.

They were so tired that they had to sit on the ground, and they even asked Sariputra for help. He then preached to them about the "Four Noble Truths": the nature of suffering, the accumulation of suffering, the extinction of suffering, and the elimination of suffering. When the workers heard this, they became filled with an inner awareness and they submitted themselves to Sariputra willingly. After that, the construction continued smoothly and finished on time. Now, we see the following line at the beginning of many sutras: "Thus have I heard. One time Buddha was at the Jetavana Garden in Sravasti..."

Jealousy is a hard habit to break. Some people become jealous when they see others being successful. Some people feel uncomfortable when they see others being praised, and they wish that they themselves were the ones being praised. Some even praise themselves and denounce others. Why? Because of jealousy. Many people are like this. People in the past were the same: when they saw others being successful, they would attempt to interfere. During the construction of the Jetavana Garden, there were many obstacles which originated from the jealousy of the local religious cult. But in the end, the cult members were persuaded and submitted themselves willingly.

A Young Monk's Encounter

There was a diligent young monk who was very advanced in learning the teachings of Buddha. He avidly sought the truth and his mind was frequently in a state of tranquil contemplation. However, a mind is sometimes like the waves on the ocean: when a strong wind blows, it can turn wild.

One day, this young monk went out to beg for food. When he entered the city, he saw a group of well-dressed women. As he looked over the group, his eyes fell on a beautiful young woman with an attractive body, face and dress. He became totally lost in her beauty. He continued to stare at the group of women until they walked out of sight.

After that, the image of the young woman and her companions continued to float in his mind. He thought about them day and night, and he lost all interest in his usual daily activities. He ate without noticing the taste. He was unaware of his warm straw mat. He didn't shave his hair or trim his fingernails. His mind was always on those women. His friends couldn't bear to see him go on like this. "What's the matter with you? Why are you so listless? You weren't like this before. What's happened to you?" Prodded by his friends, the young monk finally admitted his problem. "I'm so ashamed of myself because I'm attracted to women, and their images are rooted in my mind. I'm in pain and don't know what to do."

They felt sorry for him, but they didn't know how to help him either, so they suggested that he talk to Buddha. He didn't dare to do this, so they pulled and dragged him to Buddha. Buddha saw his haggard appearance and asked, "What happened?"

One monk replied, "He's attracted to women and he doesn't know what to do about it."

Buddha then asked the young monk, "Is that true?"

The young monk raised his head and stared fixedly at Buddha. Buddha encouraged him, "Go ahead, speak up."

He sensed Buddha's compassion and felt shame in his mind. "It's true," he said in tears. "I couldn't guard my mind and now I'm attracted to women. I'm perplexed and unhappy. Whenever I see other people, I feel that I'm impure and can't face them. Why am I so filthy inside? I regret this so much that I'm no longer comfortable in any situation or with any person."

"If you can repent, then you can return to purity," Buddha said kindly. "The tears you're shedding now can wash away your evil thoughts. You're young and don't have a strong mind, so it isn't surprising that you still have the desires of a common person. In the past, there were monks who practiced for many years and attained the highest level of contemplation and the five supernatural powers. Yet even they became lost because they couldn't resist feminine beauty. You've been a monk for only a short time, so the brief appearance of this common desire is nothing to worry about. Let bygones be bygones. You must face reality, regain your composure, and live together with the monks again. When you have no further anxieties, then you can resume your life as a contented monk."

When the young monk heard Buddha's words, he thought, "Buddha said that there were also monks who had studied longer than me but still became lost. I have only been learning for a short time." This comforting thought made him feel much better and the women's images suddenly disappeared from his mind. When his anxieties had disappeared, he raised his head and smiled in his usual old way. He bowed and thanked Buddha and his friends. "I won't be attracted to women any more," he said to them. "I will look after my mind and work on my spiritual formation. I hope that I can walk on the Path with a pure mind."

What Buddha taught was to walk on the Path with a pure mind. Everyone is a common, wordly person when he enters religious life, so which one of us doesn't have worldly habits? It's just that some have fewer such habits, while others can't get rid of their habits even after a long time and are continuously confused by things that happen around them. Learning Buddhism is learning that when adversities come our way, we can see them very clearly and our minds aren't influenced by them.

One of the Buddhist precepts for monks is the prohibition of sex; that is, monks cannot marry or have any sexual relations. Buddha taught us a long time ago that we have to keep our minds in check, and so there is this precept against sex. If sex were allowed, Buddha wouldn't have had to escape from the palace (remember that he was married). He could have stayed with his father, wife, and child and tried to attain buddhahood!

King Bimbasara Donates a Forest

When Buddha started to teach, the number of his disciples gradually increased and the assembly of monks slowly became larger. But their lives were still simple—they ate only one meal a day, slept under trees, had no permanent residence, and so on. One day, Buddha led his monks down from Gayasiras Mountain to Rajagrha, where there was a bamboo forest. When King Bimbasara heard that Prince Siddartha had become a buddha and was now teaching near the forest, he went happily to greet him.

When he saw Buddha, he was very happy. "I'm very glad to see that you are an enlightened saint. I recall that when you were still an ascetic monk, you promised to come back to preach to me. When I heard that you were finally here, I rushed here to greet you. I have the greatest admiration for your virtuous dignity."

"Your Majesty, I haven't seen you in a long time either," Buddha replied. "When I was traveling around looking for a wise teacher, I came to your territory and you sincerely wanted to share half of your kingdom with me. Thus I know that you can give alms selflessly. You will also have great fortune in the future."

The king said, "In my life, I have had five wishes. First, when I was a prince, I wished that one day I could become a king. That wish came true. After I became king, I wished to rule with virtue so that my people could live in peace. The second wish has also been fulfilled. My third wish was that a saint would appear in this world and that I would be able to see him. Now I see you, so this wish is also fulfilled. The fourth wish is that you can instruct me. My fifth wish is that I will not only hear your teachings, but I will also comprehend them totally and deeply experience the Truth."

The king continued, "Today it seems that I will be able to fulfill all these wishes. 'Human life is brief, and there is nothing that I possess.' I fully comprehend your teaching, but now I also have another wish."

"What is it?" Buddha asked.

"I hope that you will accept me as a lay disciple." Buddha immediately agreed.

The king said again, "I have another wish—I hope that you and all your monks will come to my palace for a meal." Buddha also agreed to this request. That was the first time that Buddha accepted a king's invitation.

The next day, the assembly went into the palace and the king, as Buddha's disciple, sincerely offered them food. After the meal, the king said, "Buddha, I'm very joyful because all my wishes have been fulfilled, but now I have one more wish."

"What is it?" Buddha asked.

"You and your assembly of monks have no permanent residence. Isn't this difficult for you? When you first came to my kingdom, you lived in that bamboo forest. Do you really like that place? I would like to donate that forest to you and your monks."

Buddha was very happy. "From the time we first met until now, you have always had this selfless mind. Since you have the commitment to joyfully give this forest to us, I'm very happy too."

From then on, Buddha and the monks lived in the forest. Many people also went there to hear Buddha preach. One elder noticed that Buddha and the monks got wet when it rained. He felt sorry for them, so he asked Buddha, "May I be allowed to request other followers to build houses for you and your monks as an offering?"

Buddha asked the monks their opinions. Everyone was quite happy about the idea, so rooms were built, one after the other. Altogether sixty rooms were built. This was the first permanent residence for Buddha and his monks. Because Buddha's followers enjoyed listening to his teachings, they built the monks' rooms and offered food and other donations. This all came from a spirit of joyful giving. It also allowed Buddha's teachings to remain in the world to educate all living beings.

Buddha's Noble Truths

uddha was born in this vulgar world, and he had the wealthy, fortunate life of a prince before leaving home to become a monk. However, he also noticed the differences between the four castes and the unfair treatment of the lower castes. Therefore, instead of seeking his own sensual pleasure, he wanted to find a way to spiritual deliverance for all people. He longed to explore that true meaning which transcends normal human values. He wanted to find the Truth, and he wanted to find the path out of this world.

When Siddartha was in the palace, he went through a very long struggle. He had a father, aunt, wife, child, government and country. He had to bear many responsibilities. When he vowed to leave home, how much inner struggle had he gone through? Why would his family let him go? Before he left home, his relatives had known that he had this desire and they were perplexed. Finally, the prince used his wisdom to break the bonds of fame and family.

When Siddartha left the palace, the news quickly spread through the whole kingdom. There was an aristocratic person named Purnamaitrayaniputra, son of the imperial preceptor. He had often thought that since King Suddhodana was the ruler of the realm, the prince would be the next ruler, just as he himself would be the imperial preceptor after his father (in India at that time, social status was inherited). But he saw that even someone as exalted as the king was still busy every day. Purnamaitrayaniputra's own father was the imperial preceptor, and yet he was busy and harried every day. And what was it all for? What was the value of life?

When Purnamaitrayaniputra heard the news that Siddartha had left home, he was astonished. He really admired the prince's courage and perseverance. He had thirty good friends who often gathered to discuss Brahmanic philosophy. He was the wisest among them all. He not only comprehended the teachings, but could also lecture on them. The whole group considered him to be their leader.

The news of the prince leaving home was a spiritual shock to Purnamaitrayaniputra, so he and his friends discussed what the things of this world—from wealth, sex, fame, food and sleep to social position—could give to people. They also discussed their observations that besides birth, old age, sickness and death, nothing else was fairly distributed in the world. The group vowed to change the unfair, prejudiced concepts and social situations in the world, but how could they end competition and fighting among people? The conclusion to all their discussion was that they had to look beyond all the false illusions of human life. They also decided to leave home and become monks together. They visited many schools and finally converted to Brahmanism. They built a house near Grdhrakuta Mountain and studied there.

Prince Siddartha wandered and studied for five years and was an ascetic for six years. He finally comprehended the Truth about human life and the universe, and so he became a buddha, an enlightened one. He went to Mrgadava and brought the five monks to enlightenment. Then he enlightened the son of Yasa. The news of his teachings spread far and wide. When Purnamaitrayaniputra heard about it, he was delighted that the prince had become a buddha. He told his thirty friends and suggested that they all go to visit Buddha. When they arrived in Mrgadava, they joined the ranks of Buddha's disciples.

After they had joined the assembly of monks, Buddha spoke to the entire assembly. "All of you know that Purnamaitrayaniputra is very wise. His memory is excellent and his rhetoric is flawless. Among all my disciples, he will be the best in preaching." Purnamaitrayaniputra had only just arrived, but Buddha already put much hope in him. Buddha expected that he could use his wisdom and eloquence to spread the dharma to all living beings.

The view that this group of saints had towards the world was extraordinary. They didn't cling to the status and wealth of the world. All they thought about was the suffering of this world and how to free humans from worldly anxieties. They became monks to redeem all people. They disciplined themselves so that they could free everyone from the cycle of birth and death. These saints understood themselves and saw through human life, and so they worked diligently to rescue all suffering beings.

We Buddhists should also be like this. What is the most valuable thing in this world? There is no concrete object in this world that we can own forever, so I often say, "Human beings don't have the right to own anything, but only the right to use things." The most important thing is to seek the ultimate Truth. Only the Truth has endless, immeasurable value.

A Miser Gives Alms

In Rajagrha, there was once a very rich man. His ancestors had always given alms to the poor, but when it came to this eighth ancestor, the alms-giving stopped. The reason was that this ancestor wondered why he should waste his money by giving alms to others. He thought the family wealth should be accumulated, and he couldn't think of any reason why he should keep on wasting it.

In his palace, there was a large dining hall, inherited from his ancestors. This hall had a very large kitchen and a dining area where food used to be provided to the poor. Every three days, his ancestors would have many people cook food for the poor in the city. That was the tradition that generations of his ancestors had always followed.

The eighth ancestor thought that such charity was too wasteful, so he burnt down the dining hall. Besides this, he himself ate only pickled food and he didn't want to use even a single drop of cooking oil. Since he was so cheap towards himself, we can imagine that he was even stingier towards his wife, children and servants.

One day, he was walking down a street, and he saw an ill-dressed person sitting on a rock, happily drinking from a bottle of wine that had already gone sour. When the miser walked by, he smelled the sour wine and suddenly envied that person. "If I could have a drink of wine, it would be wonderful," he thought. "But if I drank any at home, other people would smell it and want to drink it too, then all of my wine would soon be gone." So he held firm to his decision not to drink, but enduring the thought of not drinking was much more difficult than when he hadn't thought about it at all.

Before, he had never thought about the wine in his wine cellar. Now that he remembered that wine, his stomach felt emptier and his throat felt drier. As he walked down the road, he kept thinking, "If I could just have one cup of wine, I would have a hundred times as much energy." The more he thought about it, the weaker and less spirited he became. When he finally made it back to his house, he collapsed to the floor. He was weak, hungry, thirsty, and all he could think about was a cup of wine. His wife was shocked to see him this way, thinking that he was seriously sick. She anxiously called out his name, but he replied listlessly, "I want some wine."

His wife said, "That's easy, we have so much wine in the cellar."

The miser immediately waved his hand. "No, no. I can't drink it at home. If I did, everyone would smell it and would go to steal it from the cellar. In no time, all the wine would be gone. So I can't drink it at home."

His wife said, "Then why don't you drink it in the attic?"

"I can't do that either. I should drink it in the forest away from the house. I want you to get a sealed bottle of wine. Then make some food for me. Remember to cover it properly so that nobody will be able to smell it. Then bring the food and wine to me in the forest." Shrugging her shoulders, his wife did as he said.

The miser walked into the forest. He looked around and saw that there was no one around. Then he called his wife to bring out the wine and food. All by himself, he enjoyed the delicious, oily meal and the wine. He was content because no one else had even smelled anything.

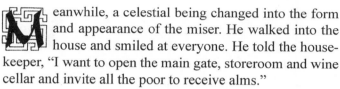eanwhile, a celestial being changed into the form and appearance of the miser. He walked into the house and smiled at everyone. He told the housekeeper, "I want to open the main gate, storeroom and wine cellar and invite all the poor to receive alms."

The housekeeper and all the servants looked at each other in amazement. When he saw the wife, the deity also told her, "I want to give alms." She was also astonished. She thought that his heart had probably been softened by the meal and the drink. She happily took out the keys and asked the housekeeper and the servants to open the granary, the wine cellar and the treasury. The deity also told her to beat a drum in the city, announcing that he was going to give alms.

Ever since the miser had inherited the wealth from his ancestors, no poor people had gone to his house. When they heard that he was going to give alms, all the poor in the city came to the house, and the wine, rice and money were soon given away.

Those who received donations went home very happily. Some of them walked past the forest. "We have to thank him," one said. "The items I received today will last me a lifetime." Another said, "His family has been compassionate since the time of his ancestors, so it's no wonder that his house is so rich." "I thought that this eighth descendant was a stingy old miser and had ruined the merits his ancestors had accumulated," another person said. "But I never thought that the day would come when he would open his storerooms and give alms. All along, his idea was to give alms after he had accumulated even more wealth." And so they continued to praise the rich miser.

Actually, he was drunk in the forest, but when he heard so many people praising him, he suddenly awoke. He rushed home and saw the front door standing wide open and empty rice bags and wine barrels scattered all over the place. He became furious and shouted, "Whose idea was it to give alms?" When everyone saw the master suddenly acting this way, they were quite stunned. He continued shouting as he entered the house. Suddenly, he saw another person who looked exactly like him sitting in his chair. The stingy master yelled at him, "Why are you in my house? Why did you give my money away?"

The one sitting in the chair said pointedly, "Who are you? This is my house!" "Who says so?" the stingy one retorted angrily. "This house is mine. Get my wife here and she can tell you who her husband is."

When she came out, she was astonished to see two persons who both looked exactly like her husband. She wondered why these two looked the same. But the one sitting in the chair was kind, gentle and compassionate, and he was able to give alms to bring happiness to others. She said, "The man sitting there is my husband."

The miser saw that his wife didn't recognize him, so he called the housekeeper. "I ordered you to do bookkeeping every day, and I was in contact with you every day. Tell me who your master is."

"Of course, the one sitting there is my master. His ancestors were kind and gentle, and he behaves like his ancestors. He is my master."

The stingy man immediately asked the servants, "Who's your real master?"

All the servants felt that the kind person who allowed them to eat and drink their fill was their real master.

The miser felt that his hope had died. His wife, housekeeper and servants wouldn't recognize him! He thought that only the king could make the decision, so he rushed to the palace and reported the affair to the king.

The king felt that this affair was quite incredible, so he called the other master to appear before him. The celestial being came to the palace and acknowledged the truth. "The real master isn't me, but him. His ancestors were kind and helped the poor in the city. However, this descendant didn't know the merits passed down from his ancestors. He became stingy and didn't use the wealth properly, thus violating the virtue of his ancestors. I considered this wrong, so I wanted to teach him a lesson on behalf of his ancestors, hoping that he would continue their traditions and look after the poor people in the city."

The miser felt quite ashamed of himself. He realized that people only had the right to use things, and that they couldn't possess anything forever. He used to ill-treat other people, so when he himself had a problem, no one wanted to help him. Then, what was the use of hoarding all the wealth? He suddenly realized that he had to use his wealth properly to build up good relationships with other people. He then vowed before the king, "From now on I'll be someone who will protect the kingdom and help the people."

Human beings don't own anything, but only have the right to use things. When we use things properly, we will be happy; but if we cling to our claims to own things, we will be in pain.

Buddha said, "In human life, what is a 'cause'? What is a 'result'? Between the two the most important thing is the 'condition.' We must build up good relationships with other people. We must also constantly do good deeds so that we can have good results." For example, a person plants a fruit seed ("cause"), which will grow into a fruit tree ("result"). But in order for the seed to become a tree, there should be water, sunlight, air and nutrients ("conditions") for the seed to grow. If any of these conditions isn't met or is insufficient, the tree won't grow at all or won't grow up properly. Thus in Buddhism we often talk about cause, condition and result.

In this story, even though the miser's ancestors had already planted many seeds of good fortune, if he himself didn't know how to create good conditions, the results could be dreadful. We must take good care of our current good conditions. We must use our good seeds properly and manage our good conditions well, then we will be able to receive good results.

The Beautiful Queen Mallika

ne time, Buddha was preaching in Mikita, and many local people accepted his teachings. Commoners, businesspersons, and people of high social status all came to listen to him. Even Queen Mallika and her servants came, and they became followers of Buddha. Queen Mallika abided by his teachings, and she even observed the fast after noon on the first and the fifteenth of every lunar month.

There was a trader named Vari, who often went abroad to do business. One day, he had just set off to sea when suddenly the sea god appeared and blocked the ship's path. "If you can answer my question, your ship can pass," the god said to him. "Otherwise, you must return."

Vari said, "Just state your question."

The god scooped up water in his hands and asked, "Is there more water in the sea or in my hands?"

"In my opinion," Vari said, "there's more water in your hands."

"There's so much water in the sea," the sea god observed. "Why did you say there was more water in my hands?"

"If the water in your hands is pure, clean springwater, it can save people," Vari said wisely. "When people are thirsty, only the water in your hands can save them. Although there's so much seawater, it can't be used when people are thirsty or hungry. So, the water that can save

life is the most useful, better than all that useless water."
The sea god was quite impressed, so he happily took out
a bag made of precious materials and jewels. The bag
wasn't only beautiful, but it was also quite valuable. No
other worldly treasures could compare with it. After the
god gave it to Vari, he disappeared and the ship went on
its way.

ari pondered the sea god's gift. "How can I
accept such a valuable item? What right do I
have to own it?" So he decided to present the bag
to King Prasenajit. When the king received it, he was also
astonished at its beauty. Who could keep it for him? Of
course it should be one of his wives, but he had so many
wives. Which one should it be? So, the king told all his
wives about the treasure, and he told them to dress themselves up, so that he could decide who the most beautiful
woman was. Then the king would present the gift to her
and ask her to take care of it.

The king's wives flew about the palace, putting on
their most elegant dresses and makeup. When they all
assembled before the king, he couldn't tell who the most
beautiful one was, because no matter how he judged
them, each one always had some shortcomings. Suddenly
the king realized that someone was missing—Queen
Mallika. He asked his guard, "How come Mallika isn't
here?"

"Your Majesty, today's the fifteenth," the guard said.
"It's the day when she always fasts. She doesn't wear any
beautiful clothes when she's fasting, so she isn't here."

The king was annoyed. "Her fasting is more important
than my command? Tell her to come immediately."

When Mallika heard that the king wanted her to appear, she insisted that she wouldn't go. "I can do as the king commands on any normal day, but there's only one fifteenth day in every month. I have waited so long for this day." She insisted on her rule of abstinence and wouldn't go to see the king.

The king waited for a long time and still Queen Mallika didn't appear. He became furious and commanded her to come before him. When she heard that the king was in a rage, she went to the main hall without any makeup or elegant clothes.

When the king saw her, his eyes opened wide. He had been dazzled by all the beautifully dressed women milling about in the hall. Mallika, however, had come in with simple, dignified clothes and a clean face. Normally he didn't consider her especially beautiful, but why was she so beautiful today? The king happily gave her the precious bag.

Mallika was surprised to see the present. "How can I accept this? As a woman, I already have so much bad karma. Furthermore, I only enjoy life here in the palace, and I don't create any good fortune. What right do I have to receive such a rare, valuable gift?"

"I wanted to give this to the woman that I love the most," the king said. "You're the one I love the most, so I'm giving this to you. Otherwise, who else should I give it to?"

A thought came to Mallika's mind. "You want to give it to the one you love, and I want to give it to the one I respect the most. If you love me the most, you will grant me this wish."

"OK, if it is your wish, then I will grant it to you."

"I want to give this to Buddha. The most difficult thing in this world is to have a buddha preach in our kingdom and thus allow the citizens to live in peace. So I want to present this bag to Buddha in order to receive great merit."

The king thought that this was reasonable, because he had heard that even many government ministers went to hear Buddha teach, and that he had changed many people and made their society become more harmonious. So, the king agreed to Queen Mallika's request and went to visit Buddha. When they saw him, they prostrated themselves before him and offered him the precious bag. The king then asked him to teach. The king was so moved by Buddha's sermon that he immediately became his disciple.

We know from this story that everyone seeks "beauty," but beauty isn't something that can be put on and worn. Real beauty comes from our hearts, and simplicity and purity can best show our beauty.

No matter how people decorate themselves, they can't prevent the coming of old age. A woman is beautiful when she's young; but when she's old, she won't be beautiful no matter how much makeup she puts on. It seems that beauty based on makeup can only fool us for a while. But if there is beauty in one's heart, everyone else will be happy to see that person regardless of his or her age, and that is real beauty. In order to obtain real beauty, we must have a pure, wise mind. Beauty based on truth and goodness is the real beauty of the world.

Five Hundred Ladies Hear Buddha Teach

In Buddha's time, there was a village by a river in Sravasti. Below a mountain near the village lived a good, righteous woman with five hundred female followers who all belonged to a Brahman religious group. She realized the impermanence and the transience of life, and she especially realized that women were quite restricted in their society. She and her followers disliked this world and had only one wish: to find a way out of this world. Therefore, they lived together and studied the principles of their religion.

The women climbed to the top of this mountain every day to collect a type of balm called "Heaven Balm." They set up an altar to worship Brahma every day. They hoped that after they died, they would go to heaven and never be born as humans again. Every day, they tirelessly toiled to the top of the mountain and they also spent a lot of money on other items to worship Brahma.

After a long while, Buddha learned about the zealousness of these women and decided to preach to them. They were persevering on the wrong path, so he wanted to show them the right path to enlightenment and liberation.

When Buddha and his disciples arrived at the village, the women were just performing their worship. These women saw Buddha's grace and radiance and thought that he was Brahma, so they immediately worshipped him and asked for his blessing.

At that, a god looked down from heaven. "This isn't Brahma," he said. "This is Sakyamuni Buddha, the instructor of the three realms and the beloved father of the world." These women had never heard of Buddha before or known that such a saint existed. Now Buddha appeared before them and they heard his name, "Sakyamuni Buddha," so they prostrated themselves before him.

Buddha said to them kindly, "I haven't seen you all in a long time!"

The women were quite puzzled. "We've never seen him before. Why would he say that?" But they were like lost children who had wandered outdoors for a very long time and now suddenly saw their dear parents. They began weeping, asking Buddha to save them and to accept them. Buddha accepted them as his disciples and preached to them. Many of them were enlightened on the spot.

Buddha's disciples saw these women and pondered, "Why are they so fortunate that Buddha himself should arrive here to preach to them? And how is it that so many of them can understand his teachings and become enlightened? This is so incredible." Everyone was especially puzzled by Buddha's statement that he hadn't seen the women in a long time, so they asked Buddha to explain. Buddha said, "When people meet the Buddha, it is because of causes that were created in their previous lives." Then he began to tell them about the past.

At the time of Kyasa Buddha, there was a very rich man. He was probably the richest man in the world. He had many servants and his wife had five hundred ladies to serve her.

His wife clearly knew right from wrong. She knew that people should do good deeds. If anyone didn't follow the rules, had an evil mind, or behaved improperly, she would treat that person like an enemy. Therefore, she and her five hundred ladies lived within their own world and hardly ever came in contact with the outside.

One day, the king invited his ministers and the elders in the city to his palace. When this rich man received the invitation, he said to his wife, "This is the king's invitation, so I have to go." He asked his wife to go with him, so she and the five hundred women followed the rich man to the palace.

The king revered Kyasa Buddha, so he also invited the buddha and his disciples to the palace to preach to all the people he had invited. The rich man's wife was delighted to hear the buddha speak. After the buddha had finished his sermon, he looked at her. "This woman is so elegant. Her mind is righteous and she knows right from wrong. If she practices her moral cultivation, one day she will be a buddha too!"

She was overjoyed to hear this and bowed to the buddha. "Buddha, do you mean that I can do moral cultivation?" she asked. "Who can teach me?"

Kyasa Buddha had a wise, compassionate disciple who diligently upheld the precepts and who had already saved many people. The buddha pointed to that disciple. "Look at him! In another reincarnation, he will be Sakyamuni Buddha. If you cultivate yourself diligently and continuously, then you will meet him in that time and he will teach and enlighten you and all those with you." That disciple heard what the buddha said, and he was also extremely joyful.

Sakyamuni Buddha finished his story. "That was the cause that was created in our past lives," he said to his disciples. "I saw these five hundred women in Kyasa Buddha's time. From that time until now, it has been an immeasurable period of time. That's why I said, 'I haven't seen you in a long time!'"

When the disciples heard this, they finally realized that everyone always meets each other for a reason.

The Archer Prince

The king of a small country had two sons. The older son was good-looking and his skill at archery was superb. He was also good in literature and martial arts, so he won the respect of all people.

The second son was totally different. He was an arrogant, jealous good-for-nothing. Although both sons had the same parents, their personalities were totally different. The king knew this, so when he grew old, he announced that he would hand the throne over to his older son.

However, the prince didn't care about high rank. He thought of his brother's jealousy, and he was afraid that the whole kingdom would be thrown into chaos if he became king. He didn't want to damage his relationship with his brother or even start a civil war. Therefore, he refused to accept the throne, even after all the ministers had spent hours trying to persuade him. There was nothing the old king could do but let his second son take the throne.

After becoming the new king, the second son was unhappy because all the people in the kingdom respected his older brother, but not him. At the same time, there were some villainous ministers who stirred things up by telling him that the prince was buying the hearts of the residents, and someday he would certainly attempt to overthrow the king. So the new king vowed to get rid of his brother. He commanded that the prince be arrested and immediately executed!

The king's guards heard about this and ran to tell the prince. The prince didn't know what to do, because he had already refused to be king. He only asked for a peaceful life for himself and the citizens of the kingdom. He couldn't believe that such a simple wish couldn't be fulfilled. He wasn't concerned for his personal safety, but he cared very much about the peace of the kingdom. Therefore, he decided to flee his country.

The prince carried his bow and arrows to a neighboring kingdom. A minister of that country saw him and liked him very much. Although the minister didn't know he was a prince, he felt from his appearance that this was a trustworthy person. So he invited the prince to the palace to see the king. The prince only asked for a place to live, and because the king liked him too, he hired him as a guard.

After that, the prince stayed on in that kingdom and worked as the king's bodyguard. However, the king's other guards became jealous of him. They had no idea where this new guard came from, but they saw that he was highly regarded by the king. They were unhappy about this and planned to get rid of him.

One day, the king and his guards went to enjoy the scenery in a garden. The king was tired from walking and rested under a tree. He saw some ripe fruit on a tree branch and an idea came to his head. "Look, that fruit is ready to eat," he said to his guards. "If anyone can shoot down an entire bunch, I'll reward him handsomely." All the other guards knew that this was their chance. "We still don't know how good this foreign guard is. Now is a good chance for him to show us his skill."

The king said to the prince, "Can you do it?"

"No problem, Your Majesty," the prince said. "This is easy. Do you want to see the arrow flying downwards or upwards?"

"I've always seen arrows flying upwards. I've never seen anyone shoot downwards."

"OK. It will take some time for my arrow to come down. Can you wait?"

"I'm really looking forward to seeing an arrow flying slowly downwards."

So the king pointed to a cluster of fruit and the prince shot an arrow. It went straight through the center of the bunch from below and went out the top. Then it turned around, came straight back down and neatly cut the stalk. The entire cluster of fruit then fell to the ground. Everyone was amazed. They didn't know whether they should look at the fruit, the arrow or the stalk. Such skill was indescribable. After that, nobody bothered the new guard anymore, and he stayed in the palace in peace.

Meanwhile, after that new king took the throne, he didn't know how to govern the country well. He continued to be arrogant, and his people became angrier and angrier. When other countries heard that the older prince had fled, they decided to swallow up this small kingdom.

When the young king heard this news, he was very frightened. He didn't know what to do. He normally acted very brave, but now that disaster was about to strike, he was terrified. He thought, "If my brother were here, everything would be all right." And so he started searching for him.

A minister heard that there was a skillful archer in a neighboring state, so he went to look for him. When the minister saw the archer, he realized that he was their prince. When the prince heard the news, he was quite concerned, because he still cared about his people and his state. So he asked the king to allow him to go back to his own country.

The young king saw his brother returning and embraced him happily. He told the prince about his problems. The prince comforted him and said, "Don't worry; I have an idea."

The prince went up to the city wall and shot an arrow toward the enemy camp. The arrow flew far and landed in the center of a dining table in the camp. At that time, the seven kings that had formed an alliance to swallow up this small country were having a feast and planning for the next day's attack. The kings and their armies were surprised to see an arrow appear out of nowhere and land on their table. They saw a slip of paper on the arrow. "The prince has returned," it read. "I ask all the kings to stop their attacks."

The kings realized the troubles they would face if they carried out the assault. They decided to withdraw, and the small kingdom escaped disaster. The younger brother also realized his mistake and decided to hand over the throne to his brother. But the prince refused to accept it. "What I love about you is your repentance. I hope you can get rid of your jealousy and love others with an open mind." His younger brother was very touched and loved his brother even more. He asked his older brother to assist him in governing the country. After that, other kingdoms never again dared to attack this small country.

This story tells us that we must take a step backward when dealing with other people. When we love others, we must open our hearts. We must have a mind as vast as the universe.

Section 3
THE RESULTS OF
KARMA

What is "happiness?"
Actually, it exists in a single thought.
Heaven and hell arise from the mind.

The Queen's Honor

ne day, Buddha and his assembly of monks were traveling through a small kingdom. The king venerated Buddha very much, and when he heard that Buddha was passing through his country, he sensed that this was the chance of a lifetime to encounter this great teacher. So he went to welcome Buddha and the monks at the border. He was very polite and sincere when he met Buddha, and he invited Buddha and the monks for a meal in the palace. Buddha agreed, and he and his disciples went to the palace.

The king's servants carefully prepared the meal, and Buddha and his disciples were able to enjoy many delicious dishes. The king also called his wife to greet Buddha and his followers. When she entered, the queen sincerely bowed to Buddha. However, when the monks saw the queen, they were bewildered.

After the meal was over, Buddha gave a sermon, and then he and the monks left to continue their journey. Halfway down the road, they rested under a large, leafy tree. The disciples sat around Buddha. "When we were eating and the queen came into the room, I noticed that you all looked puzzled," he observed. "Why was that?"

"This is a small kingdom and this king is the ruler of this small kingdom," one monk replied. "But after all he is a king! Why is he married to such a fat, sloppy woman? That really puzzles us."

Buddha smiled. "Don't you know? The most important thing in life is a sense of honor. The cause for the karmic relationship between the king and his wife is that one of them had this sense of honor." The monks were still confused, so Buddha told them the story.

When the queen was quite young, she went out one day and suddenly felt the call of nature. The locals were used to relieving themselves anywhere that was convenient. However, she was quite fat and it wasn't easy for her to squat down, so she found a higher piece of ground to relieve herself.

Suddenly she heard the king passing by the place where she was. She at once covered herself with a piece of cloth. When the king went by, he noticed her. He thought that this girl really had a sense of self-respect, and she knew enough to cover herself at a time like this. Since she had such a sense of honor, if he married her, she could set a good personal example and assist him in ruling the kingdom.

The king then asked his attendant where this girl lived. The attendant went into the village and asked some questions. When he discovered where the girl lived, he reported back to the king. The king sent someone to the girl's family to propose marriage.

Buddha said, "It was just that simple. It all happened because of a small gesture of honor." This girl had a sense of honor, so she covered herself with a piece of cloth. The king respected her for her sense of honor and self-respect, and he married her simply because he had an intuition that she would be a good example to his people. After she entered the palace, the girl, who was originally quite sloppy by nature, became fatter and fatter. Therefore, when the monks first saw her, they wondered why she was so fat and untidy. Buddha said, "The point is that because of her sense of honor and one small gesture, she became a queen."

There is a saying: "One thought creates three thousand merits." If we are mindful of a single virtue, such as propriety, justice, honesty or honor, and if we put it into action with even one small gesture, it can affect our whole lives. The turning points in our lives often depend entirely on our tiny actions from minute to minute. When the time is right, these small actions may bring immense good fortune. Therefore, we must constantly cultivate our sense of honor. Honor comes from a pure, undefiled heart, and with such a heart, we will never feel ashamed.

In short, we must learn to be good people. When we no longer have any faults, we will gradually reach buddhahood. If we have any shortcomings, it will be hard for us to become buddhas. Some may say, "Since it's impossible to have no faults, doesn't that mean that it's also impossible to be a buddha?" No, that isn't true. Anyone with the will can accomplish anything! It's like the queen whose tiny action brought her such good fortune. We should not consider any thought or action to be insignificant, not even one pure, good little thought, because such actions and thoughts accumulate to bring good results.

A Story About the Result of Karma

A highly-respected monk went traveling and studied at many temples. One time, he was staying at the Wakuan Temple. Every day, he prostrated himself before the Lotus Sutra and studied it thoroughly.

One night, he suddenly felt the need to relieve himself. When he reached the washroom door, he saw a ghost standing there. The ghost instantly bowed down before him. "Why are you guarding the toilet?" the monk asked the ghost. "You seem quite sincere. What caused you to become a ghost?"

The ghost wept as he knelt on the ground. "I was once a monk too, and I was in charge of incense and receiving guests. I accidentally broke some precepts, so after I died I became a dung-eating ghost. I know that you, venerable monk, have great achievements. Only with your strength can I be saved."

The monk then asked him, "What did you do?"

"I'm not sure," the ghost replied. "I must have broken some precepts to become like this. I just don't know which precepts I broke."

"No matter which precepts you broke, they are all based on what you do, say and think. Did you break the precepts against killing, robbing or sexual conduct?"

"No. After I became a monk, I never broke these precepts."

"Did you break any precept of speech, such as uttering lies, improper remarks, double-talk, or abusive speech?"

The ghost thought for a while. "I didn't break the precept against lying, but I had an abusive tongue, double-talked, and used flattering words."

"Did you break the precepts of mind, such as anger, greed or delusion?"

The ghost thought for a while. "Greed could have been my problem. When I was in charge of incense and reception, I had to talk to many people. Sometimes temptations arose in my mind, and I stole some offerings of oil and money. Greed might have been my biggest crime, but I couldn't control my anger either. I also had delusions, because my wisdom wasn't well-developed, and I was often anxious about different things. So, I believe my punishment was due to errors in my speech and in my thought." He now realized what his mistakes had been.

The ghost earnestly wanted to repent. "I know I was wrong, so I'm asking you to create some merit for me," he said to the monk. "I hid $3,000 under a persimmon tree in the temple garden. I hope you will take the money and hold a religious service for me so that I can be saved." The ghost disappeared and the monk went into the washroom.

The next morning, the monk called some people with their hoes to the persimmon tree, and they dug up an urn. Inside he found the money. The monk then used the money to make a copy of the Lotus Sutra, and he donated the rest of the money to the poor. A week later, the ghost came to his room and bowed to him. "Thank you very much for what you did for me. My karma has been altered, and I'm better than before. I'll work unrelentingly, hoping that I can be freed from this ghostly form and return to the human realm." The ghost then disappeared.

The process of life is so mysterious that common people cannot comprehend it. When we create merit, how much good will come of it? When we create bad karma, what kind of results should we expect? Learning Buddhism is understanding that our lives are shaped by our previous actions, whether they are good or bad. This is what we need to understand in our moral cultivation— you reap what you sow.

The Monk and His Mother

When Buddha was preaching in the Jetavana Garden, a young man constantly went there to listen to his sermons. He felt that Buddha was wise and that his teachings were wonderful, so he studied tirelessly. His mother wasn't happy about this. She was suspicious of the Buddha and his teachings, and she didn't want her son to be so close to the Buddha. However, she cared for him very much, and for his sake, kept her opinions to herself.

One day he said to her, "I want to be a monk."

His mother couldn't take it any more. "As long as I'm alive, you cannot be a monk," she said firmly. "You must concentrate on your job and earn a lot of money. You can become a monk after I die. Now you must just think about working and don't get too close to Buddha."

He was a good, filial son, and so he agreed to her request. Buddha taught us to be filial to the "living buddhas at home"—our parents—and the young man followed this teaching. As long as his mother was alive, he would care for her lovingly.

He worked hard day and night to make money, but his mother was reluctant to spend any of it. When monks came to their house to ask for food, she didn't give them any and she even insulted them. When beggars came to their house, she would often ask a neighbor to beat them. She was stingy and disliked almsgiving.

Whenever her son brought home some money, she had it changed into golden coins. To keep the coins safe, she

buried them in the ground all around the house. No matter
how much money her son earned, she would always com-
plain that it wasn't enough. The son never complained,
and worked hard for his mother. He was patient with her
stinginess, even though he didn't like it.

Years later, the mother finally died from an illness.
Although he grieved the death of his mother, the young
man—no longer so young—could finally fulfill his desire
to become a monk.

He went to Buddha's assembly and was welcomed
there. He became a monk, and dedicated all his energy to
developing spiritually. For nearly ten years he studied
hard. One day, he found a clean place and asked Buddha
to let him build a hut and study there. Buddha agreed, and
the monk built a small hut. He spent all his days alone,
immersed in study and meditation.

One day, a dirty, poorly dressed woman came to
his door. Her whole body was hideous, as if it
had been burnt by fire. She prostrated herself
before the hut and wept. The monk came out and asked
her, "Where are you from? Why are you like this? Why
are you crying?"

She said, "Venerable one, don't you remember me? I
was your mother twenty years ago. Because I was stingy
and jealous of saints, I prevented you from being a monk
and I also created much bad karma for myself. After I
died, I fell into the realm of hungry ghosts, where I suffer
all sorts of agonies. Only you can help free me!"

He felt very sorrowful upon hearing this. He had never
thought that while he had been living as a monk, his
mother had been suffering in the realm of hungry ghosts.

"What can I do to help you?" he asked her.

"Give alms with all my money," she said. "Then I can be free."

He didn't know that she had hidden all the money. "What is there to give?"

"I buried the money all around the house. You can dig it up and donate it to the poor and to the monks."

He went immediately to do what she asked. He dug up all the money, and then used it to buy food and daily necessities. For forty-nine days, a stream of poor and hungry people came to the hut and took what they needed. The monk quickly gave away all the family property.

One evening, his mother, appeared to him. She was dressed in white like a celestial being. She thanked him for creating merit for her and freeing her from the realm of hungry ghosts. She could now enter the heavens.

Buddha used stories of contemporary people to educate future generations. We normally take money from society, but we should also use it in society to create more merit.

A Brahman Asks for the Buddhist Dharma

Buddha met all sorts of people and all sorts of religious believers. He also had to solve many of their problems. If anyone raised a question, he would answer in detail. He taught about the realm of nirvana and he instructed his disciples how to enter it. All his disciples aspired to this achievement, while others were curious about what nirvana was.

There was a Brahman, a member of India's priestly class, who respected Buddha's character and who could also accept his teachings. He even hoped to enter nirvana, so he often went to listen to Buddha's teaching. One morning, he came to Buddha and prostrated himself. "Buddha, the nirvana you talk about is my aim and my goal. But I'm not sure I understand what it is. How can I achieve liberation from this world? After I die, how can I enter nirvana? How can the soul be free? And where does the soul go afterwards?"

Buddha responded, "In my belief, nothing comes or goes and nothing is created or destroyed."

Hearing this, the Brahman was confused. "How so? Does a human still live in this world after he dies?"

"Human nature never changes. It is neither created nor destroyed. That is the realm of freedom." The more the Brahman heard, the more confused he became.

"Since you don't understand my answer, then I'll ask you a question in return. If a piece of wood is burning and someone asks you why there is fire, how would you reply?"

"I'd answer that he can see the fire because the wood is burning."

"If the fire goes out and someone asks you why it went out, how would you answer?"

"I'd answer that the fire went out because the wood was burned up."

"If someone asks you where the fire goes after it goes out, what would you say?"

"I'd say that he asks too many questions! A piece of burning wood naturally makes fire. Once the wood is used up, the fire of course goes out. This is a natural process. Why would anyone ask where the fire went?"

"Yes, and it's the same with humans," Buddha said kindly. "People's anxieties stem from having these bodies and from having to deal with all sorts of people and affairs in this world. Because of our six sense organs of eyes, ears, tongue, nose, body and mind, we make distinctions in our perceptions of the world around us, and this brings us anxiety. If we eliminate our anxieties—that is, if we do not cling to our sensory perceptions, but turn them into wisdom—then we will be able to alter our environment with wisdom!

"In short, it is our bodies and senses that cause our anxiety to flare up. If we are clear about our senses and perceptions, then the flame of our anxiety will be extinguished. Once there is no anxiety in our hearts, our souls will be free and at ease. When the mind no longer bears anxiety in dealing with the world, that is nirvana! Nirvana is not someplace else that we go to after we die. Nirvana is freedom, and a clear, tranquil mind is nirvana."

The Brahman finally understood. Yes, if we leave the here and now, where can we go to seek nirvana? If we abandon our daily life, where can we look for liberation? Without the anxiety and suffering of this world, there would be no nirvana. Anxiety and nirvana are related to each other like opposite sides of a coin. It depends on how you look at it.

If you can deeply experience Buddha's teachings, then no matter what situation you are in, your mind will have no anxiety, and no matter what you perceive, you will have no desires.

In your daily life, if you can clearly recognize your true nature and truly develop your abilities, you will have no anxiety. If you can do this every day, your life will be clear and bright, and that will be nirvana. If you seek freedom and nirvana, you can find it in the here and now. When your mind is without darkness, but instead is pure and free, that moment is nirvana.

Four Things in This World That Can't Be Ignored

he foundation of being a human being is courtesy. We must respect the elderly and the wise and should not look down on youngsters. When Siddhartha was enlightened, he was only around 30 years old. The Jetavana Garden was only just finished. Whenever the residents of Sravasti heard that Buddha was coming to the park, they would joyfully go there to hear his sermons.

At that time, King Prasenajit from the kingdom of Kausala heard that Buddha was preaching in the garden. He went there thinking that this enlightened saint must be very old.

When he prostrated himself before Buddha, he saw that Buddha was still so young. He wondered if this young man of only 30 could really be enlightened. So he asked, "Buddha, are you truly enlightened? Can you really free us from all human suffering?"

Buddha replied kindly. "Your Majesty, there are four things in this world that you cannot ignore: a young prince cannot be ignored, young dragons and snakes cannot be ignored, a small fire cannot be ignored, and young novices cannot be ignored."

Buddha explained. "When a young prince is born, you know that in the future he will ascend to the throne and govern the country, so you cannot look down on a prince even when he is still small. A dragon has the power to control the wind and rain, and we need these for a peaceful life. If the rain comes in due season, everything will flourish. Untimely rain only creates disasters, and no rain at all brings drought. A dragon has the power to control the weather and the rain, so it cannot be ignored even when it is young.

"Although snakes are small, a poisonous one can kill with a single bite, so even a young snake cannot be taken lightly. A tiny fire can become a large, uncontrollable blaze, so it cannot be disregarded either.

"You cannot neglect novices either, because they diligently study the sutras and absorb many teachings. In the future, they will be great monks who can educate the people to relieve their suffering. So, do not ignore novices or young monks."

After listening to these words, the king felt Buddha was right. He realized that he shouldn't look down on others. He had to be attentive not only to major affairs, but to minor ones as well. Big things grow out of little things, so what is small shouldn't be ignored. From then on, the king respected Buddha very much, and he later became a disciple and a great supporter of Buddha.

We Buddhists must always feel grateful and respectful towards others, young and old. "Seniority" can be a matter of old age or experience, but we must respect it either way.

On the other hand, experienced or elderly people cannot slight the young either. Some old people feel that because they are old or have more years of experience, they can bully or sneer at youngsters. They say, "I've eaten more salt than you," or "I've crossed more bridges than you." This is not the correct attitude.

More experienced people should care for less experienced people. The elderly should care for the young as they would their own children. The social order that Buddha wanted us to build is "respecting the elderly and caring for the young."

Vimalakirti's View on Almsgiving

imalakirti was a very famous lay follower of Buddha. Although he was a householder and not a monk, he was said to have a buddha's wisdom and eloquence. In fact, many of Buddha's disciples, and even some bodhisattvas, couldn't debate with him.

One day when Vimalakirti was sick, Buddha asked some of his disciples to visit him, but no one wanted to go. The reasons they gave were basically the same: Vimalakirti could really talk, and none of them dared to visit him, or they would be lectured.

There was a zealous, devout lay follower named Shanhui. One day he went to listen to Buddha preach. Buddha hoped he would go visit Vimalakirti, because he was young and wise. However, Shanhui did not want to go either, and Buddha asked him why. He told of his experience with Vimalakirti.

One time, Shanhui held a feast. He gave food to all the monks, and he also gave alms to the poor, the handicapped, beggars, and so forth. The feast went on for seven days. Vimalakirti passed by his house one day and said, "This is not real almsgiving."

Shanhui asked, "Then what is real almsgiving?"

"Just giving money is not enough—you should also offer the dharma."

"How can I offer the dharma?"

"You must give rise to kindness by means of bodhi heart, compassion by means of saving all living beings, joy by means of supporting the true dharma, and generosity by means of cultivating wisdom."

What did Vimalakirti mean? "Give rise to kindness by means of bodhi heart." "Bodhi" means the Path or Way. We must be committed to the Buddhist Way and give rise to kindness by means of the Way in our hearts. Kindness is giving happiness. We should give happiness to all people without any distinction or prejudice. Making people happy shows our bodhi heart.

"Give rise to compassion by means of saving all living beings." Once you have opened your bodhi heart, you will think about how to rescue all creatures from suffering. This is compassion. Whenever you see creatures in pain or discomfort, you will try to help them. Thus, saving all living beings gives rise to compassion.

"Give rise to joy by means of supporting the true dharma." If you want to give joy to everyone, you can't simply give them material things or try to make them feel good. You should also try to give them correct concepts and thoughts. This gives them something that they can keep forever. We should not only show compassion and try to make everyone happy, but we should also motivate others to preserve their compassion, get involved and give of themselves. Then they will find great joy.

There is a saying, "To give is better than to receive." If we can guide people to give with a correct, pure mind, they will receive perpetual joy. This is the true dharma. They will not go astray, and they will be content and happy.

What is suffering? What is happiness? Poor people don't necessarily suffer just because they don't have money. People who are rich or have high social status are not necessarily happy either. Suffering and happiness are only in the mind. If people are poor but content, they will always be happy. This is the true dharma. So we have to give rise to joy by means of supporting the true dharma. Once we have the right concepts, not only will we always be happy, but we will also be able to influence other people to give happily and to share their joy.

"Give rise to generosity by means of cultivating wisdom." Wise people know that if they do not cling to things, but continually give of themselves, they will have no anxieties and they will be happy. In order to motivate everyone to cultivate their wisdom, they must have this generosity.

This shows that anyone who walks the Buddhist path can be happy. No matter where one goes, that place will always be a training ground for the mind. Each environment will always have some undesirable features, but if one always remembers that each place is a training ground, one can transform that environment.

If we concentrate on our work, we'll never have any anxieties. We'll always have a feeling of accomplishment. A mind that is committed to the Way is thus a training ground, and it is also the bodhi mind. With this bodhi mind, we are always happy and at ease. We often talk about "kindness, compassion, joy and unselfish giving." "Kindness" is charity work, "compassion" is eliminating suffering, "joy" is changing our way of looking at the world, and "unselfish giving" is education. Our daily life cannot part from these four concepts. Carrying out these concepts cultivates good fortune and wisdom.

Vimalakirti Overcomes the Enemy

When Buddha was on earth, he was the leader for the monks, nuns, arahats and bodhisattvas, as well as male and female lay followers. One of Buddha's disciples was Dharanimdhara Bodhisattva. One day he was meditating when suddenly Mara, the king of all evils, and 12,000 beautiful women appeared and prostrated themselves before him. Mara had disguised himself as Indra, the emperor of heaven, so Dharanimdhara unsuspectingly welcomed them.

"You planted many seeds of good fortune in your past lives," Dharanimdhara said to Mara. "Therefore, you can now enjoy good fortune and lead all the gods. However, you shouldn't lose yourself in your enjoyment. You should know that such happiness doesn't last. Instead, you should quickly create good fortune for all human beings."

"Because of my great fortune, I want to give happiness to other people," Mara said. "Will you accept these women?"

Dharanimdhara shook his head. "I'm a monk and cannot accept them."

"Don't worry about it. They can sweep and clean the place for you, and they can also sing and dance and give you anything you want!"

Dharanimdhara didn't know what to do. Suddenly, Vimalakirti appeared. "Mara! Dharanimdhara can't accept your women, so why don't you just give them to me? I'll be happy to take them!"

Mara was shocked to see him. "That is the king of all evils, not the emperor of heaven," Vimalakirti told Dharanimdhara. "He's here to shake your commitment to the Way and to destroy your wisdom!" He turned again to Mara. "Don't you want to give these women away? I want to have them!"

Mara was scared and wanted to run away, but he couldn't move because of Vimalakirti's extraordinary power. As he struggled, Vimalakirti said to him, "I'll let you go if you leave these women behind." Mara did so and escaped.

Vimalakirti said to the women, "Sit down and listen to me." The women obeyed their new master and sat down quietly. "Human desire is unlimited," he told them. "In order to be free from the five desires for things seen, heard, smelled, tasted, or touched, you must have four faiths. When you have gotten rid of the five desires, you will have permanent joy. The four things you must believe in are Buddha, his teachings (the dharma), the monks, and the precepts."

"Faith is the mother of all merits," he continued. "If you want to be Buddhists, it will be extremely difficult if you don't have firm faith. So first, you must believe in Buddha. You must understand the greatness and wisdom of Buddha and wholeheartedly accept each of his teachings. You must believe in every single word and never forget it. Then you will have a firm faith in the dharma. The next is the faith in the monks. Buddha will not live in this world forever, so after he passes away, the assembly of monks will lead us. Besides believing in the dharma, we should also respect and have faith in the monks. They preach the dharma to all, and you must sincerely accept and abide by the dharma. Finally, you must have faith in the precepts. The monks take the precepts as their teachers. If you can follow the precepts, remove all evil and cultivate the good, you will be free from the cycle of reincarnation and you will receive eternal joy.

"The precepts are the first condition for removing the five desires. Human beings create evil because of their attachment to the five desires. They can't control their minds and thus create evil karma. If you want to stop evil and attain eternal happiness, you must believe in the precepts, abide by them, and be free from the five desires."

When the women heard Vimalakirti's sermon, they were filled with joy. They thought, "Even if we lived in heaven and enjoyed heavenly bliss, we would still have anxieties, because we would still have our desires and fears. But Vimalakirti's preaching makes us feel the boundless joy of the dharma!"

Faith is the mother of merits, so we must have faith in Buddha, the dharma and the monks. Believing in them means that we have to stop evil and avoid creating any more evil, and this is keeping the precepts. If we keep the precepts, of course we won't create evil karma, and so we'll be pure and free.

The Two-Headed Bird

An old monk asked Buddha why Devadatta, who was Buddha's cousin and disciple, had turned against Buddha and continually spoke against him. "I can't help it," Buddha said, and he told this story.

Long ago, there was a two-headed bird. The heads took turns resting, so one head could always be on the lookout. Actually, one head was awake and on guard most of the time because the other one was always asleep. When they ate, the alert head would wake up the sleepy one to eat. When it was time to rest, the lazy one fell asleep again. The other one never complained and always stayed on guard.

One day, the lazy head said, "I want to sleep now, so you be on guard." As it fell asleep once again, a breeze suddenly sprang up and blew down a fruit from a nearby tree, which then rolled to the bird. The fruit was ripe and smelled ever so good. The alert head thought, "The other head is asleep, so I don't want to wake it, but it will still enjoy the fruit even if I eat it." So it ate the fruit.

The sleepy head suddenly smelled the fragrance and heard the sleepless head burp. It woke up and asked, "What did you eat? How come your burps smell so good that they woke me up?"

"It was a ripe fruit," the alert head said. "I didn't want to wake you up, so I ate it myself."

The sleepy head wasn't happy. "Why didn't you wake me up to enjoy it? All right, I'll get even someday." After that, its mind was filled with hatred.

A few days later, the lazy head said to the other head, "Today you can get some rest and I'll stand guard." The alert head happily agreed. When it was asleep, another fruit blew down from the tree, but this time it was a poisonous fruit! The sleepy head thought, "All right, I'll eat this one and we'll die together!" With a heart full of hatred, he ate that poisonous fruit.

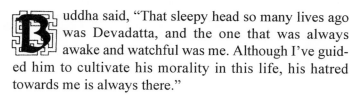 uddha said, "That sleepy head so many lives ago was Devadatta, and the one that was always awake and watchful was me. Although I've guided him to cultivate his morality in this life, his hatred towards me is always there."

After listening to this story, we know that the most difficult thing to control is the mind. Devadatta was Buddha's cousin and disciple, but Buddha still couldn't teach him the first thing about controlling the mind.

The most important thing in spiritual formation is yourself. When you truly want to cultivate your morality and work hard to remove anger, greed, delusion, suspicion and arrogance, only then can you get rid of your anxieties. Otherwise, even if you were reborn as a bird with two heads, you would still have evil thoughts of hatred and revenge, which would harm both yourself and others. How sad that would be!

The Beautiful Antlers

here was a beautiful deer who roamed the most beautiful areas in the mountains. Every day, he ate and drank without a care in the world.

One day, he came to drink at a clear, clean lake. When he came to the water, he saw the reflection of his antlers. The branches of the antlers criss-crossed in a lovely pattern, and they looked like a beautiful tree. He now realized that he was so elegant and he was very happy about that, but he also became quite proud.

After drinking the water, he lowered his head and saw his four legs. The thin, spindly legs annoyed him. How could such a beautiful head and antlers go with such ugly legs? He despised himself.

Suddenly, he heard the sound of hunters. He was frightened and ran away as fast as he could. But in his flight, his antlers got caught in some tree branches and vines. His life was in danger, but no matter how he struggled he couldn't free himself from the tangle of branches and vines. At that moment, he realized that what put his life in danger were the beautiful antlers that he had been so proud of, but what could have saved his life were his ugly legs. But now his antlers were caught...

Buddha told this story to teach us that human beings should have a balanced mind. We shouldn't be egoistic, arrogant or self-centered. We should maintain our composure and not get nervous. We should also respect ourselves and others. We should happily accept the kind of body our parents gave us. We shouldn't doubt or despise ourselves, nor should we be arrogant. Buddha taught us to always be level-headed, which is also a good way to protect ourselves.

Therefore, learning Buddhism is learning self-composure. We should learn Buddha's great wisdom with a balanced mind, and our anxieties will then be under control. No matter what kind of situation we are in, we must learn to accept things as they come to us and keep our minds steady.

The Drum and the Fox

Buddha spent a period of time preaching in the Jetavana Garden in Sravasti. "You must watch over your bodies and your minds," He often said to his disciples. "If you cultivate your morality but break any of the precepts, then you won't attain any degree of wisdom. We cultivate morality in order to cultivate wisdom, and in order to obtain wisdom you must start by abiding by the precepts."

Buddha told a story. "There was once a good drummer, and he had an excellent drum whose sound could travel thousands of miles. But after a long time, the drum head finally broke. The drummer wanted to repair it, so he stitched on a few layers of cowhide. When he was finished, the drum didn't sound very good. He didn't know what was wrong, so he again added more layers of cowhide, but the sound became more and more dull."

"Why was that so?" Buddha asked the disciples. "The drum was originally made with cowhide, which was quite proper, but why did the sound become so dull?"

The monks replied, "The sound was dull because he was unwise and didn't know how to repair the drum properly."

"That's right," Buddha said. "It's the same with spiritual formation. You won't gain wisdom if you don't know how to go about it. So I want you to abide by the precepts in order to guard your minds and manifest your wisdom. All karma comes from the mind. If your minds have bad thoughts and you act upon them, you will receive much suffering in the future. So you must abide by the precepts. If you follow them strictly, you will become compassionate and dignified. Otherwise, how will you be able to help others? Therefore, you must maintain decorum and abide by the precepts. Everyone hopes to eliminate bad karma, and to do that, you must first cultivate your minds and get rid of your muddled and evil thoughts. So don't keep thinking about the past, because the past is confusion. Don't think about the future either. The best time for spiritual formation is every moment of the here and now."

here was another story. Buddha asked the monks if they had heard a fox howling the previous night. The monks said, "Yes, it howled so sadly."

"Do you know why? In his last life, the fox was a monk, but when he was meditating, even though his body was still, his mind wandered everywhere. One time, the sound and the shape of a fox arose in his mind, so after he died, he was reborn as a fox. Now whenever he thinks about his current existence as a fox, he howls unceasingly."

Buddha continued. "The most important thing in cultivating morality is to cultivate wisdom, bringing the body and the mind together. When you are in meditation, you cannot physically sit still and let your mind be full of thoughts and fantasies. If you cannot control your mind, you will fail."

It is clear that spiritual formation is not a matter of external appearances. The most important thing is to abide by the precepts. The proper ways of walking, standing, sitting and sleeping all start from abiding by the precepts. True spiritual formation is to be done at every moment. If a person's body is here but his mind is in the past or the future, then his mind is muddled and confused. Everyone must remember: the precepts are our rules. We must pay close attention to our behavior. If we let our attention wander even a little, the results may be unthinkable.

In this world, we don't have the right to own anything, but only the right to use things. We must grasp every moment and work hard. In our cycle of reincarnation, it is rare to be born as a human, difficult to hear the Buddhist teachings, and hard to follow the Path of the Bodhisattvas. Since we are human beings and can hear the Buddhist dharma, we should diligently follow the Path of the Bodhisattvas so that our lives won't be wasted.

The Elephant and the Dog

Among Buddha's disciples, there was a monk who used to go to a friend's home every day, and he always had his meals there. After they finished eating, the two would chat until sunset. The friend would then walk with the monk back to the monastery, but they would continue talking. They didn't seem to want to part. When it was quite dark, the friend would leave to go back home, but this monk would accompany his friend back to the city. They did this every day, and many people were curious as to why they were such close friends.

One day, the monks were talking about it when Buddha walked in. He saw them chatting, so he asked, "What are you talking about?"

The monks reported the situation. "Their friendship wasn't built up just in this life," Buddha observed, "but it is a result of karma that was accumulated in the past." He then told the following story.

Long ago, there was a king who liked a certain elephant very much. He hired a mahout (an elephant keeper) to take special care of it, and he fed the elephant with the finest food. One day, a small dog appeared from nowhere. At first, the dog always stayed far away from the elephant. When the elephant had its meal, it would drop some rice to the ground. The little dog then approached the elephant slowly and carefully to get the rice. As time went by, they became familiar with each other. The dog would come every day, and when the elephant saw it coming, he would always drop some food for it. They became good friends, and the dog would come and stay with the elephant every day. They both liked each other very much, and they played happily together every day. The dog would even climb up on the elephant's head, and the elephant would hold the dog with its trunk. In short, they became inseparable friends.

After a couple of years, someone came to the stable and saw the elephant and the dog playing together. "This dog is so cute," he said to the mahout. "I also have an elephant at home, and I want to buy this dog for my elephant." The mahout was only responsible for the elephant, but now someone wanted to buy that dog and he could make a profit from it! So he sold the dog. But from then on, the elephant was very depressed. It wouldn't eat or drink, and it groaned as though it were ill. The mahout was quite worried, so he reported it to the king.

The king immediately ordered a minister to find out why the elephant was ill. This minister was very wise, and when he saw the elephant, he knew that there was no problem with the elephant's health. But why wouldn't it eat or drink, and why did it keep groaning? He asked the mahout, "Has this elephant had any emotional changes in its daily life?" The mahout then told the whole truth about the little dog and how it had been sold. The minister asked, "Where does this person live?" The mahout said, "I don't know." The minister reported his findings to the king. "The elephant isn't sick. It is simply that it suddenly lost a close friend." He suggested that the king post an announcement that the person who bought the dog should return it.

A few days after the announcement was posted, the dog was indeed sent back. It was delighted to see the elephant and climbed up on its neck and head, and the elephant once again happily held the dog with its trunk.

Buddha concluded his story. "Although they were animals then, their feelings towards each other continue today. The dog is now that monk, the elephant is his friend, and I am that minister. The monk and his friend are still very dear to each other because of the karmic relationship that they built up in their past lives."

The Fire of the Senses

O ne day, Buddha was leading more than 1,000 monks to beg for food when they approached Gayasiras Mountain. This place stirred up many memories for Buddha. From the top of the mountain, he looked off into the distance. "If you look towards the northeast from here," Buddha said to his disciples, "you can see the streets in the city of Gaya. To the east is the Nairanjana River, and farther away is the place where I studied, did my spiritual formation and was enlightened. When you look down from here, the mountains and rivers, cities and forests, and everything in the world is on fire." However, all the disciples saw was tranquillity. Why did Buddha say that everything was on fire?

Buddha noticed that everyone was puzzled, so he explained. "My disciples, now listen carefully. Human eyes burn, the ears burn, the nose burns, the tongue burns, and most importantly, even the mind burns. For example, the eyes are attracted to appearances, and in the desire for appearances the mind cannot be in peace. The ears hear something and the mind is attracted to the sound. The nose and the tongue cling to smell and taste. Due to the craving for the flavor of food and drink, the mind cannot rest in a pure state. In sum, in everything the body comes in contact with, we look for physical enjoyment, and thus we create bad karma.

"All these desires come from the mind. The fires of anger, greed and delusion continually burn in our mind, so the five organs—eyes, ears, nose, tongue, and the body—continue to suffer. The senses and the mind keep on burning, so this world is never in peace. The fires of greed, anger and delusion are destroying us."

Buddha's way of teaching was to use examples from daily life. Human reactions come from the five senses. When we encounter something with our senses, our minds react, and we feel either anger, greed or delusion. Because of these emotions, our mental processes and our behavior go astray, like wild fires destroying everything.

Every day, we can open the newspaper and read disturbing reports of disasters caused by the fury of the fire in the mind. Recently there was a shocking story. One day, a homeless wanderer got drunk and had a quarrel with an eleven-year-old boy, during which the homeless man kicked the boy once. The youngster felt that he had been mistreated and wanted to get revenge. So he found three junior high school students who always skipped school and told them that he had been bullied and beaten. He told them that he was angry and hoped that they could help him get even.

The four of them went to look for that homeless person, and at one o'clock in the morning they found him, still dead drunk. They got some sticks and rocks and started to beat him on the head. Of course, the homeless person tried to defend himself, but he was no match for the four of them and he finally died from loss of blood. In the morning, some workers discovered the body and reported it to the police. The police worked hard to find out who did it. Someone said that a youngster had had a quarrel with the dead man. Following this lead, the police caught the truant junior high school students, and from them they found the instigator.

The main culprit of this incident was an eleven-year-old! He and the three fourteen-year-old youngsters created such a tragic, cruel incident. When the police asked him if he regretted what he had done, he answered that it was too late to regret it. He was frightened by the results, but it had already happened. Their parents were shocked and sad, unable to believe that their children could kill anyone.

How could something like this happen? It was because of the fire of anger and the fire of delusion, both created by unhealthy minds. So Buddha said, "Human eyes burn, the ears burn, the nose burns, the tongue burns, and the mind burns. The fire of greed, the fire of anger and the fire of delusion are burning." All of these are capable of destroying us, so we must always be alert.

A Monk Learns to Follow the Precepts

A young man thought about how Buddha used to be a prince, but gave up his wealth and became enlightened. Now he was respected by all the people in the world. The young man hoped he could leave home and follow Buddha, so he asked for permission from his parents. They didn't want to part with him, but they were Buddhists too. They looked up to Buddha very much, and they also respected the monks Finally they sent him to Buddha, asking Buddha to fulfill his wish.

Buddha accepted him and asked a senior monk to instruct him. The senior monk then informed him about their daily rules and precepts. When the young monk was told to follow the five precepts, the ten precepts, and even the two hundred and fifty precepts of the monks, he got scared. "A monk has to keep so many rules," he thought. "If I'm not careful, I'll break one very easily. I don't think I can abide by all the precepts, and since I can't do it, I might as well go back home. I can have a business, get married and have kids, and furthermore I can support the monks too!"

When he told the senior monk about his decision, the old man felt uneasy. Buddha had entrusted him to look after this novice, but now the young man wanted to go home. The senior monk didn't know what to do, so he told the young man, "Of course you can return home, but you must tell Buddha about your decision."

The senior monk then went with this young man to see Buddha and inform him about his decision. Buddha asked him, "Why are you going home when you only just became a monk?"

"Everyone here must abide by the precepts, but there are so many of them," the young man replied frankly. "I'm afraid that if I break one, I'll dishonor the order of monks. Wouldn't that be awful? So I want to go home and find a job, and this way I can help support the monks."

"You've changed your mind just because you heard so many precepts?" Buddha said. "Why do you have such a weak will?" Buddha turned to the senior monk. "Why did you scare him by telling him so many precepts all at once? You should teach him gradually. Let me talk to him."

The young man felt much better. Buddha spoke to him kindly. "Young man, spiritual formation is not as difficult as you think, and abiding by the precepts is not as horrible as you think either. Just forget about all those precepts and follow the three that I'm going to tell you now."

The young monk heard that there were only three. "Three? That's easy. I can do that."

"Now I want you to listen carefully," Buddha said. "I just want you to be mindful of your actions, words and thoughts. If these three are pure and clean, then you can keep all the precepts." The monk heard this and was quite delighted. He bowed to Buddha and vowed to abide by the three precepts for the rest of his life.

Buddha turned to the senior monk. "Now I'm entrusting this young monk back to you. You must teach him well." So the young monk abided by the precepts every day, and because his actions, words and thoughts were pure, he was happy every day. After a while, he attained the arhathood. Many monks who heard about this praised the wisdom of Buddha, because he could enlighten a person with a few simple words. He was able to simplify the complex precepts and make them easy for the young monk to follow.

Simplicity is beauty. Learning Buddhism is not so complicated. If we can have a simple life, then is there anything we cannot accomplish? And why can't we be happy at everything?

Whenever I go to Taichung, some little children always come to visit me with their piggy banks. One child started this when he was only two years old, and now he's almost four. He hasn't started kindergarten yet and he's really adorable. Last time, he came to see me with his piggy bank as always. When he saw me, he said, "Master, this is for you to build the medical college. I bow three times before your picture every day. Do you see me? And do you hear what I tell you every day?"

"What do you say?" I asked.

"I hope that I can say nice words, do good deeds, and think good thoughts. I say that to you every day." Do you hear that? A little child can make this wish every day! If we can be innocent, say good words, do good deeds, and think good thoughts like this child, is there any precept that we cannot follow?

Section 4
THE PATH OF THE BODHISATTVAS

The goal of all Buddhists is to become a buddha,
but we all begin as common human beings.

The Brahman's Test

Once, Buddha was preaching in Sravasti. One young man came to him. "I teach mathematics. There is a rule in math and that is that you must perform your calculations according to correct, orderly teachings. Now I want to ask you: when you are teaching your disciples, are your teachings also correct and orderly, or do you just follow your own rules?"

"Young man," Buddha answered, "when I instruct my disciples, I follow ordered principles and the rules of reason. It's like this: if I want to train a horse, I must first train it to go in the right direction, and then I can continue to train it to do other things. Later on, when the horse runs on the road, it will know the right direction."

The young man continued. "The nirvana you talk about is so wonderful, but does such a beautiful place really exist? Has any of your disciples ever been there? Is there anyone who has been taught but still cannot attain nirvana?"

"Yes, nirvana really exists," Buddha said. "It's a glorious place of spiritual tranquillity and physical and mental liberation. As for whether anyone has ever reached nirvana, I believe that anyone who studies and works hard can enter that state. Of course, there are also people who haven't reached nirvana. Those who are lazy, idle and inattentive cannot go there."

The young man persisted. "Buddha, you are the teacher for human beings and heavenly beings. Why is it that some of your followers can reach nirvana and some cannot?"

"Young man, suppose someone asked you how to get to Sravasti, and you told that person which road to follow. If that person went in the wrong direction or took a wrong turn, what would you do?"

"I did my best to tell him where to go, where to turn, and so on. If he makes a mistake somewhere or doesn't pay attention, that's his own problem. I'm just a guide. There's nothing I can do."

"That's right! In the same way, I'm only a guide to the correct path. I do my best to direct my disciples. Whether or not they listen attentively or have the ability to go the right direction on the correct Way, it all depends on them."

From this story, we can understand that Buddha has done his best, and it's up to his students to be attentive. It's not enough just to teach through the scriptures. One must also teach through one's own personal behavior. The best educator can teach both by word and by example. If you cannot teach the scriptures, you must still teach by your own example.

The worries and troubles that arise from dealing with other people can discipline us and give us a chance to learn how to remove those worries and clear up our minds. But how can we let go of our spiritual anxieties? How can we stay pure even in the midst of all the troubles of the world? The answer is that we must be attentive at every instant.

Wise People Stop Rumors

When Buddha was enlightened, he first took in five monks, and later he took in another fifty young men who had followed Yasa. Later, more and more people came to be his disciples, and very rapidly the total number of his disciples reached more than a thousand. If you read the Amitabha Buddha Sutra, you will find the phrase "together there were a thousand two hundred and fifty people." This phrase is used in sutras to indicate the greatness of the order of monks.

Buddha and his disciples traveled and preached along the banks of the Ganges. One day, they reached the city of Rajagrha. They stayed in a monastery and went into the city to ask for food. But when they were in the city, they noticed that everyone was whispering excitedly to each other. What were they talking about?

Those who feared the coming of Buddha and his monks had started a rumor. The rumor was that wherever Buddha went, many of the best and most capable people, young and old, would become monks. Therefore, parents were afraid that their sons would leave home, and wives feared that their husbands would become monks. The rumor upset everyone in the whole area.

So, when the monks went to ask for food from married women, the women would quickly close the doors. Parents of sons would also shut their doors tight when they saw the monks approaching. It was this way throughout the whole city. The rumor kept spreading from house to house, and every resident was terrified. One morning before they set out, the monks reported all this to Buddha. "The rumor won't last long," Buddha said to them. "It will go away in seven days at most. If we act and speak properly, the rumor will disappear very quickly, in no more than seven days." When the monks heard Buddha say this, they felt better and continued to go out and ask for food.

Seven days passed. During these days, the people of the city saw Buddha's dignified appearance and heard his sermons. Buddha spoke of the four types of disciples [monks, nuns, male and female lay followers] and the regulations of monks and laity. The people were then aware that Buddhists didn't have to become monks. Lay followers didn't have to abide by the 250 precepts of the monks, because the laity had only their own five precepts to follow. They could live a Buddhist family life. There were ways for lay followers to develop spiritually. The people of the city were satisfied. The rumor disappeared, and the locals admired and respected Buddha even more. Once again, they happily gave food to the monks.

From this story, we can see there's a human tendency to believe rumors, and so rumors spread quickly. However, Buddha felt that if his actions, words and thoughts were correct and if he stayed calm and continued to teach patiently, any rumor about him would simply disappear in a matter of time. His actions show how "wise people stop rumors."

Modern society is full of suspicion and conflict. As Buddhists, we should learn Buddha's spirit and act, speak and think correctly. We should also learn that whenever we hear a rumor, we must ignore it and stop it right there. Then our lives will be happy, and we will not get caught up in disagreements.

The Spiritual Craftsman

Buddha's disciples came from all sorts of back-grounds. In Sravasti, there was an able young man who was barely twenty years old. He was good with music, board games, literature and art. He was also skillful in medicine. But the more he learned, the less satisfied he became, and so he was never happy. He vowed to learn all the skills in the world.

He traveled around looking for teachers. He learned everything. He wanted to be sure that he would always have good clothes to wear, so he became a skillful tailor. So that he would always have good food to eat, he also became an excellent chef. He could do things that nobody else could do, but he was still unhappy and dissatisfied. So he vowed to leave Sravasti and travel all over the world to learn every kind of skill imaginable.

He saw someone making bows and arrows. The crafts-man's movements were skillful and quick, so that a bow was quickly finished and every bow was the same size. The young man thought the craftsman must be very accomplished. The young man wanted to learn this craft, so that if anyone attacked him, he would have something to defend himself with. He worked hard until he became even better than his teacher.

Then the young man saw a sculptor carving a piece of wood to produce a dragon that looked like it was alive. He thought this was a good skill to have, so he threw himself wholeheartedly into learning it, and soon became an excellent woodcarver. Traveling further, he saw someone building a boat. He felt that he had learned many skills that would be useful on land, but what if he needed to cross a river? So he learned how to make a boat. He traveled through sixteen countries and mastered many crafts.

When the young man returned to Sravasti, he was very arrogant, because he felt that he had mastered all the skills and crafts in the world. Thinking to show off his skills, he posted an announcement inviting all to come compete with him in any skill they chose.

When Buddha heard about it, he went to the man's house. The young man saw Buddha and some of his disciples approaching, and he thought they were quite strange. He had seen all sorts of people, even kings, but he had never seen anyone with such strange robes and shaved heads. He wondered what kind of people they were.

He approached Buddha curiously. He was attracted by Buddha's dignified appearance, and he instinctively folded his hands together. "Sir, where are you from? What class and profession are you in?"

Buddha replied, "Bow and arrow makers flourish when they are close to bamboo forests. Sculptors prosper when they live near forests. Boat builders are successful when they are close to the sea. But a wise person is skilled in regulating his own mind and body."

The young man became even more curious. He had traveled and learned all the skills and crafts in the world, but he had never heard of a skill in regulating the mind and body. He asked Buddha, "How many ways are there to regulate the mind and body?"

Buddha said, "There are the five precepts, the ten virtues, the six perfections and the four noble truths, and the three freedoms.* These are all methods of regulating the mind and body."

The young man did not know what these were and he was curious.

Buddha said kindly, "One person cannot eat all the rice in the world, and one person cannot do everything in the world. In this world, we must each use our own special talents to support each other. We should always be grateful and always repay other people. If you can be grateful to other people, to your parents, and to heaven and earth, then your mind will grasp the five precepts and the ten virtues. After that, you can understand more deeply the four noble truths and practice the six perfections to bring out all your potentials."

When the young man heard this, everything became clear to him, and he entered into deep contemplation. It was a beautiful world that he had found, so he asked Buddha to accept him as a monk. He studied very hard, and before long he became an arhat.

---

*The five precepts: no killing, no stealing, no lying, no fornication, and no drinking.
The ten virtues: no killing, no stealing, no fornication, no lying, no double-talking, no abusive words, no improper remarks, no greed, no anger, and no delusions.
The six perfections: charity, moral conduct, patience, devotion, contemplation and knowledge.
The four noble truths: existence is suffering; suffering is caused by human passion; suffering can be eliminated by the destruction of human passion; human passion can be ended by a life of holiness.
The three freedoms: everything is formed by conditions and has no ego or self; everything is impermanent and has no real form; since everything is impermanent, we have no desires, and are thus free from the cycle of reincarnation.

In sum, one person cannot do everything, just as one person cannot eat all the rice in the world. We have to be grateful to other people, to our parents, and to heaven and earth. Then, our minds will be good and joyful. No matter what kind of environment we find ourselves in, it will always be beautiful.

The Ugly Princess

There once was a king who had a daughter. She was very ugly and bad-tempered, so when she was old enough to be married, no one in their social class wanted to marry her. It was very embarrassing for the king, and he didn't know what to do. Finally the king announced that as long as a man had a good background and wasn't a slave, even if he were poor, he could marry the princess.

One day, a young man wandered into the kingdom. He came from a good family and seemed like a suitable choice, and he was willing to marry the princess. After they were married, they got along well with each other. One day, the young man decided to take his new wife back to his hometown. The king was delighted and gave them chests of gold and expensive gifts to take to the young man's family. The king also ordered bodyguards to escort them. The husband went home proudly and all his relatives and friends came to celebrate. They felt that their household was honored and they wanted to see what the wife looked like.

However, the young man made up all sorts of excuses why they couldn't meet his wife. He even locked the door so that no one could force their way in. His relatives and friends felt this was very odd and thought, "Why can't she come out to see us?"

The princess passed the days in sadness, and she felt wretched every time she saw herself in a mirror. She tried to hang herself, but the rope broke in half.

She was overwhelmed with emotions. She realized that suicide wouldn't solve anything. It would be an offense against her parents and would bring many troubles to her husband. With so much misery in her heart, she cried bitterly.

t this point, she suddenly thought of Buddha, so she folded her hands together and, facing the place where he lived, she sincerely and devoutly prayed. Perhaps because she prayed so intensely, she seemed to see Buddha talking to her. "In your previous life, you gave alms joyfully, so in this life you were born into a royal family and enjoyed all sorts of luxuries. However, because of your violent temper, you beat your servants for any little thing and you treated others with anger. Therefore, you became ugly, and everyone who sees you is frightened. You create your own fortune, good or bad. You must repent wholeheartedly, think about the majestic, dignified appearance of Buddha, think about the suffering of all beings, and cultivate your compassion and love. This will solve your problem."

After hearing this, she earnestly contemplated Buddha's compassionate appearance, and she spoke and acted towards others with kindness.

One day, her husband was drunk. Everyone wanted to see what the princess looked like, so they slipped his keys from his pocket and entered his house.

When the door was open, they admired the princess's upright, dignified silhouette. Their curiosity satisfied, they went back and woke up the husband. "Congratulations! Not only are you a king's son-in-law, but your wife is also beautiful."

The husband was quite puzzled to hear that. She was certainly ugly, so how could they say that she was beautiful? He ran into her room to take a look.

Although her appearance hadn't changed, she had become well-tempered, modest and gentle, so that she seemed to be kind and attractive. It was like seeing two different people. This is what is meant by the Chinese saying: "One's appearance comes from one's mind."

Pure Love

ne morning, Buddha's monks were talking excitedly with each other. Buddha approached and asked, "What are you talking about?" One said, "Something really touching happened in the city." Buddha said, "Tell me about it."

ome people were going through the forest near the city when they were set upon by three robbers. The people defended themselves, and the robbers ran away. Those people chased after the robbers, but quickly lost sight of them and didn't know which way they went. They continued to look around, and then they saw three farmers working nearby. They thought that the robbers were pretending to be farmers to avoid capture. So they seized the farmers and brought them to the king, even though the farmers pleaded their innocence.

Not long after the three farmers were caught, a woman came to the palace, crying and begging to see them. The guards wouldn't allow her to see them, and they pushed her away. After that, the woman kept crying outside the palace and shouting, "Give me something to cover myself, please give me something to cover myself!" She cried bitterly for hours.

Inside the palace, the king heard her. "That woman is crying again," he said. "Give her a piece of cloth to cover herself."

A guard gave her a piece of cloth, but she said, "I don't want a piece of cloth to cover myself."

The guard returned and told the king, "She said that she doesn't want this cloth."

The king was curious. "If she doesn't want this cloth, then why does she keep shouting outside? Tell her to come in."

The woman came in. "What you need is a piece of cloth," the king said. "Why didn't you want the cloth I gave you? What do you need to cover yourself?"

"Husbands are the covers for their wives," the woman replied. "If a woman doesn't have a husband, it's as if she were naked. She can put on a lot of clothes and adornments, but she would still be naked and have nothing."

"Where is your husband?"

"By mistake, my husband was brought here earlier as a robber. He's innocent, and we are simply law-abiding farmers. He is jailed here in the palace."

"Three people were brought here a couple of days ago. Which one is your husband? Who are the other two?"

"One is my husband, one is my son and one is my brother."

"All right, you can choose one to set free."

She thought for a while and finally said, "Then please return my brother to me."

"That's strange," the king frowned. "You said that if a woman didn't have a husband, it would be as if she were naked. I told you to choose one of the three men, but why did you choose your brother? Isn't your husband more important?"

"Yes, a woman must rely on her husband all her life," she replied sadly. "A woman without a husband is to be pitied. But I could only choose one of them. I thought that since I'm alive, I can still marry again. But my parents loved my brother very much. They have passed away, and in order to repay their love, I chose my brother. I know quite well about parents' love towards their children. My heart aches to know that my son is also here. Although my parents have died, their love is eternal. In order to repay my parents, I must respect their love for my brother. So I have to give up my husband and my son in order to rescue my brother."

The king was touched by the depth of her love. He couldn't find any evidence that the three men had committed any crimes, so he released all of them. The news spread all over the city.

Buddha was moved by this story. "This woman is incredible. Many people are confused by love, but she understands how her parents felt, so she gave up her husband and her son in order to rescue her brother. This transcends all normal love. She is indeed extraordinary. Her pure love impressed the king and all three men were released. This also means that if love is innocent and unlimited, it can really inspire many people."

Many of us simply look after ourselves. When a woman is married, the most important thing in her life are her husband and her son, and her feelings towards her brothers become insignificant. This story is two thousand years old, but this woman's incredible love still moves us.

There is a saying, "The mind creates all." Selfish love comes from the mind, and enlightenment also comes from the mind. Buddha taught us to clearly examine all our different kinds of emotion in order to elevate our selfish love to the love of the bodhisattvas.

Learning Buddhism is learning to treat all elderly as our parents, all those of our own age as our brothers or sisters, and all younger people as our children. This is the great love of the bodhisattvas.

The Monk Sronakotivimsa

Buddha had a disciple named Sronakotivimsa. He came from a very well-to-do family, and he became a monk because he enjoyed hearing the dharma (Buddha's teachings). He was very ambitious. It seemed to him that many disciples were enlightened as soon as they heard the dharma and quickly rose to arhathood. He was from a good family and considered himself intelligent, so he was confident that he would be enlightened very quickly. In fact, he wanted to attain enlightenment before any other disciples did.

The monk began to think a lot about enlightenment and when it would happen to him. In fact, he began to worry about it, and then he found himself becoming more and more perplexed. For a while he made no progress at all. He didn't know where to start learning, and he didn't know how to make his mind act in accord with the dharma. He was very disappointed. "Since I can't understand the dogma, what's the use of being a monk? Why don't I just stay home and be a lay follower?"

Buddha knew what Sronakotivimsa was thinking, so he asked someone to bring the young monk to him.

When Sronakotivimsa came to Buddha, he felt both grateful and ashamed. He felt grateful because Buddha knew what he was thinking and cared about him. He felt ashamed because although he was a monk, he was unable to be enlightened quickly and repay Buddha's kindness.

Buddha knew what he was thinking and spoke to him kindly. "Sronakotivimsa, you come from a good family, so you had a very good education. You're especially familiar with musical instruments. Are you interested in the lute?"

"I'm not only interested in it, but I used to play it often."

"You know music theory quite well. The strings on a lute are plucked to produce sound. If you tighten up the strings, what kind of sound is produced?"

"The strings can't be too tight, or else it won't sound good and the strings will break easily."

"What if you loosen the strings?"

"No good either, because there won't be any sound at all."

"Your mind is just like a string that is too tight. It doesn't sound good and it'll break very easily. A lute string must be adjusted just right, not too tight and not too loose. It's the same with spiritual formation. If you try to rush too fast, you'll become excessively attached to the dharma, and you may become lost in its vastness. You mustn't become careless or idle either, or else you'll become morally corrupt. You must advance at a natural speed, neither fast or slow. This will allow your basic nature to return to its original, pure condition. If you guard your six sense organs well in your daily life, you'll be all right."

Sronakotivimsa asked, "What are the six sense organs?"

"They are the eyes, ears, tongue, nose, body, and mind. If you guard them well, no anxieties will arise, and your mind will return to its original state of tranquillity."

That was how Buddha taught his disciples. He stimulated lazy disciples and cooled down overly zealous ones.

The six sense organs are important. Most of us look at the world with our physical eyes, so we tend to be confused by our desire for what we see. Those who follow Buddha should open up the eyes of their hearts and close their physical eyes. Then everything they see will be natural, pure and carefree.

Buddha and the Brahman

A Brahman went to visit Buddha, who was preaching in the Jetavana Garden. He prostrated himself sincerely before Buddha. "Buddha, I'm not your disciple and I believe in a different religion. However, I respect and admire you very much. I've learned Brahman teachings for many years, but I'm still confused. May I ask you to clarify a problem for me?"

"Of course," Buddha replied kindly. "Although you're a Brahman, all lives are equal and all teachings are related. You may ask me any question."

"Buddha, I generally consider myself wise, and I can clearly distinguish people, things and events. I can debate endlessly and everyone agrees with my analyses. However, sometimes my mind is unsettled and full of anxieties. Then, whatever I see, think, or feel is all mixed up. I can't speak clearly, so I feel extremely annoyed. Why can't I have a clear wisdom that can go on continually? Why does my mind get so unsettled?"

"Take a look at the water in this basin. If you put red, green and blue dyes in the water, can you see your face in the water?"

"Of course not. If the water is colored, how can I see my face?"

"If you heat the water on a stove until it boils, can you see your face?"

"That's impossible. When it boils, the water rolls all around and steam rises over the surface. How can I possibly see my face?"

"The water in a pond is still, but if there's a lot of green algae and leaves floating on the water, can you see your face?"

"That's also impossible. Even though the water is still, if there's too much stuff floating in it, you can't even tell where the water is, let alone see your face."

"That's right. Still, clear water is like a mirror in which all the features of your face are clearly reflected. You can see everything around you in the water too, because the water is still and clear. The same is true with the mind. When the mind has no desires or anxieties, its natural purity will appear, and then you'll be able to see and analyze things correctly. Whatever you say from the heart will be reasonable, and you'll be able to debate without any self-doubts. When your mind has desires and anxieties, it's like adding dye to the water. Since your mind is polluted with the ignorance of desires and anxieties, you certainly cannot see your original self. If your mind is still but the anxieties are still there, it's like having moss floating on a pond. Of course you still won't be able to see clearly.

"A little bit of anxiety is like the fire of ignorance. When it begins to burn, the water of your mind boils and steams. How can you see yourself clearly?"

The Brahman finally understood. The most important thing is that the mind must be tranquil and pure, and then it can be bright and reflective like a mirror. Desires are like muddy dyes, and anxieties are like fire. We must wash away ignorance and get rid of our anxieties and desires. Then pure wisdom can appear.

The Master and the Thief

n old meditation master was cultivating his morality in a hut on a mountain. One autumn evening, while he was chanting Buddha's name, a thief suddenly jumped in through the window. He went through all the drawers, turned everything upside down and made a big mess. He only found two coins, so he took them and was about to jump back out of the window.

The master knew the thief was going through all his things, but he just sat there quietly. Just when the thief was about to jump out of the window, the master opened his mouth. "Mister, mister, why don't you just walk out the door? Why do you come in from the wrong place and exit from the same wrong place? You should walk uprightly through the correct place."

The thief was startled when he heard these words. He turned around and saw that the master was calm and sincere. The thief then calmed down. When he was about to open the door and leave the hut, the master said again, "Mister, when you get something from someone, you ought to say 'thank you.'"

When the thief heard this, his heart was struck again. His greed disappeared, and he went back and prostrated himself before the master in repentance. "When you steal something, then you're a thief," the master said. "But if I give you the same thing, then I do you a favor. Don't think that you're so skillful. You must realize that someone is being kind to you."

The thief learned his lesson. He stopped stealing and, with a heart full of gratitude, he even got a job and worked very hard. When his business was successful, he became a great supporter and patron of this master.

There is a similar story from Arabia. A businessman, Mr. A, had an excellent horse which could run over a thousand miles a day. It could carry a lot of cargo, and so the master loved it very much and took good care of it. Another businessman, Mr. B, drove camels to transport his goods. He was envious of Mr. A's horse.

One day, Mr. B said to Mr. A, "I want to trade my camels for your horse."

Mr. A replied, "No way."

Mr. B said, "If you give me this horse, you can have anything you want from me."

"I don't care what you say," Mr. A said. "As long as I'm alive, I won't give my horse away. It's my dearest companion, so I can't give it to you."

However, Mr. B really wanted the horse. He also knew that Mr. A was a very loving, compassionate person. One day, he dressed up in old, torn clothes and, pretending to be ill, lay by the road where Mr. A was going to pass. When Mr. A saw someone lying by the roadside, he immediately jumped down from his horse. He saw that it was that other businessman who kept wanting to trade for his horse. Mr. B seemed to be very sick. Mr. A decided to take him to a doctor and with great effort helped him get on the horse.

When Mr. B was securely seated on the horse, he sat up straight. "I tried all sorts of ways to get you to trade your horse, but you would never part with it. Now I'm on your horse, so this horse is mine, and I'm just going to ride it away."

Mr. A said calmly, "Since you are on the horse, it is yours, but I want you to promise me one thing."

"As long as the horse is mine, I'll listen to anything you say."

"Remember, if anybody asks you how you got this horse, you must never tell him."

"Why?"

"If you tell people how you tricked me, then when anyone else falls sick by the roadside, no one will dare to help him. So for the sake of those people, you must not say a word. Let others preserve their compassionate hearts."

When Mr. B heard this, he felt very ashamed. He immediately got off the horse. "Because I got hung up on one thing, I distorted my basic human goodness. I'm ashamed of myself. Here, the horse is still yours."

This is a lesson in wisdom and compassion. Actually, there is goodness in each one of us. It's just that sometimes we can't resist temptation and so make a mistake. If we use a tranquil mind and wisdom to guide such a person, we can restore that person's basic human goodness. The important thing is that we must cultivate joyful hearts and treat others with wisdom and gratitude. In this way, our lives will be fortunate and happy.

The Lost Calf

A farmer tilled the land and raised cattle next to the monastery where Buddha was staying. One day, a cow gave birth to a calf. Days after it was born, the cow and the calf went out to graze in the pasture, but the calf wandered off and became lost.

The farmer saw the cow mooing, calling anxiously for its calf. He was quite anxious too, so he went everywhere looking for it. He searched from morning till night, day after day. Six days later, he still hadn't found it and he was worn out. At this time, Buddha was just leaving the monastery to go beg for food when he saw the exhausted farmer.

Buddha asked him kindly, "Why are you so tired?"

"I'm so worried," the farmer said.

"Why are you so worried?"

"You wouldn't understand."

"Just tell me. If you talk about it, you'll feel better."

"I'm worried because I lost a calf."

"Why do you need to worry so much just because of one lost calf?"

"I just knew it! You can't feel my worry because you're a monk."

"What do you worry about most of the time? I can't feel your anxiety at this moment, but at least you can talk about why a lost calf causes you so much worry. Just let it all out!"

The farmer thought that since he was so tired, he might as well take a rest and talk about it. "Whenever I'm worried, I look over to the monastery and see you and your monks going out to beg for food. Your lives are so free and easy. I really envy you."

"What do your problems have to do with our carefree lives?"

"Look, I lost a calf and I worry that this will affect my livelihood, because I need cows to plow my field. I have to worry about my family. I have a wife, seven sons and seven daughters. If the harvest is bad, I'll hear fourteen kids crying that they're hungry, and my wife will nag that there isn't any rice to eat and there isn't any money to buy things. I worry about so many things! But you monks don't have to worry whether there's any water in the rice fields, or whether it'll rain, or whether your kids are fed, or whether your wife has money. I really envy you."

"It sounds like you have a point," Buddha admitted. "I don't have any cattle to lose, and I don't need to worry whether my seven sons and seven daughters have food or not. I have no family to bother me. It's true that we monks have fewer anxieties, but we got this ease of mind by leaving everything behind. You yourself ask for your anxieties. But you only worry about one calf, one field and one family. Do you know that I have worries too? I worry about the great family of all creatures that live in the world. The fields that I cultivate are the minds of all living beings. The cattle that I have are those that till the fields of their minds. I want to make the cattle fat and healthy, make the field fertile, and let all creatures live in peace. Now think about it, whose anxieties are greater, yours or mine?"

"My problems really are pretty small," the farmer admitted. "They're nothing compared to your burden."

"Yes, what are your problems compared to mine?" Buddha said. "But like you, I also worry about 'have' and 'have not,' because I'm part of the whole universe and the whole universe is part of me. Nothing is permanent. We only have the use of it for a short while."

The farmer suddenly understood everything. "Losing a calf is nothing! What I got just now is something extremely special!"

Buddha once said, "Property belongs to five families." When one has possessions, one is afraid of five things: bad rulers and corrupt officials, robbers, good-for-nothing descendants, water, and fire. All these can destroy one's property. This is the anxiety caused by having possessions. Buddha talked about this in his own time, so obviously people had this kind of anxiety even then.

To a common person, "to have" is an anxiety, and "to have not" is also an anxiety. When you have something, you worry that it might be lost or broken, but if you don't have it, you worry whether you have enough money to buy it. More possessions mean more worries; fewer possessions mean fewer worries. The universe is quite fair. When we "have not," the days of our lives pass in peace and health. When we "have," we suffer the anxiety of craving even more.

Venerable Ching Chen

Before the Chinese revolution of 1911, a 99-year-old monk lived in an old temple on Sungyang Mountain. He told his disciples that when he died, he wanted them to seat his body on a chair in a cave (a common burial ritual for monks). They accordingly did so.

When the Red Guards roamed China in the 1960s, they destroyed many cultural traditions. They destroyed the temple and opened up the cave where the monk was buried. When they saw a live-looking monk sitting there, they were astonished and at once sealed up the cave. They didn't dare do any damage.

This monk was Master Ching Chen, born in a village at the foot of Sungyang Mountain. When he was twelve, his parents died in a plague. He was taken in by an orphanage. He was loved and cared for, and when he was eighteen he was quite strong and healthy. But because of his difficult childhood, he felt that life was impermanent and filled with suffering. After observing the truth of the world, he decided to become a monk.

The young man became a novice at Kai Yuan Temple. Four years later, he was fully ordained as a monk. He then went to the old temple on Sungyang Mountain to do his spiritual formation. At that time, villagers near the mountain had abandoned farming and instead hunted animals and collected firewood on the mountain. He was curious about this situation. "Why would everyone abandon farming and instead hunt and collect firewood? This not only destroys the forest, but also destroys the lives of the animals."

After some serious thought, Master Ching Chen decided to teach the villagers in two ways. On the one hand, he spent a lot of time and energy educating the villagers about Buddhism, the consequences of the Buddhist law of cause and effect, and the equality of all living creatures. In this way, the villagers could begin to respect and protect life. He used many stories to teach the villagers. He did all this because of his compassionate commitment to protect lives, hoping that people would not create so much bad karma.

At the same time, the master began raising funds to build small dams. The villagers could build irrigation canals to bring mountain spring water to the farm fields below, thus allowing farming to return. The monk's whole-heartedness, perseverance and sincerity moved many villagers to join him. They stopped hunting and chopping down trees. They also cooperated to build the dams, and after a period of hard work, they successfully brought water to the fields.

After a couple of years, all the villagers had gone back to farming and the harvest was abundant. The animals on the mountain once again led their normal, peaceful lives. Everyone was grateful, because all this had been made possible by one person's sincerity. Master Ching Chen's patience and perseverance affected many people and improved their lives. Even the birds and the animals could live peacefully. The monk was not afraid of hard work, but devoted himself physically and mentally to the people. He finally died at the age of ninety-nine, and when his body was discovered decades later, it still had not decayed.

Master Ching Chen lived like us, but he had superhuman zeal, which came from his sincerity and patience. He started when he was around twenty years old, and didn't stop until he was ninety-nine. That was dedication! I believe that because of his dedication and patience, Master Ching Chen will return soon to lead more people on the Path of the Bodhisattvas.

The Farmer and the Hoe

There was a farmer who tilled his field with his hoe day after day, year after year. He worked hard and his harvest was abundant, but still he was never satisfied. "Tilling the field every day is so boring. What does it mean? Where does life come from and where does it go?"

One day, a monk came to him, begging for food. The farmer thought that the monk looked free and happy, coming and going as he pleased. He decided to give up everything and become a monk himself.

When he walked out of his house, he suddenly felt how empty his hands were. He was so used to holding his hoe in his hands to work that without the hoe, he now felt that something was missing. So he went back and picked up his hoe. The shaft was smooth and shiny from daily use. He kept stroking it, unable to bear the thought of leaving it behind.

"All right," he thought, "I'll put it away." So he cleaned it and wrapped it in layers of cloth, and then he stored it in a secure place. Feeling better, he finally left his house.

The farmer was determined to be a good monk. He studied diligently and made a lot of progress. But whenever he saw the green plants in the fields, he would think of his hoe. He often couldn't resist the temptation to go back home and look at it. He would unwrap the layers of cloth, caress the hoe tenderly, then wrap it up again and return to the temple.

fter seven or eight years, he began to wonder why he hadn't achieved anything in his spiritual formation. After some serious reflection, he discovered that there was still something he couldn't part with. He made up his mind to break this attachment.

He went home and took out the hoe. He walked to a large lake and with all his strength threw the hoe far out into the lake. Splash! He felt as though a very heavy weight had fallen from his heart. "I've succeeded, I've won!" he shouted exultantly.

Just at that moment, a king leading his victorious army happened to pass by. He heard the shout echoing in the air, "I've won, I've done it!" Far off, he saw the unusually joyful monk, so he rode over and asked, "What have you won? Why are you so excited?"

"I battled against the evil in my mind and I won," the monk said. "Now all my attachments are gone."

The king saw that the monk was so happy and that in his heart he was truly free and at ease. "I'm a powerful king and can lead thousands of soldiers and horses into battle," the king thought to himself. "But even though I've won, do I have peace of mind? Am I happy?" He realized that his victory was not as great as this monk's. Although he had conquered another country, it was only a superficial victory.

The king really admired the monk. He felt that one who had conquered the devils in his own heart was a real saint, while one who had only conquered a human enemy was just an ordinary person.

From this we know it is very important to remove anxieties. We often say, "Forget about it, just let it go." This is much easier said than done. Because it isn't easy to do, it is called "spiritual formation." If we always stubbornly cling to our attachments, we will often make trouble for ourselves and other people.

Delusion and anxiety trap us in the cycle of reincarnation. It's like a rope that is all knotted up. In order to untangle it, we must give up our attachments. That farmer couldn't part with the hoe that he had carried every day. After seven or eight years of spiritual formation, even though the hoe wasn't in his hands, it was still in his heart. He wasn't able to be truly free until he threw it far into the lake.

The Lost Child

Buddha told a story recorded in the Lotus Sutra. A young boy from a rich family, ignoring his father's warnings, wandered off to play in a strange part of the city and couldn't find his way back home. He wandered on the streets for years, enduring every kind of suffering. His father left their home and searched everywhere for his lost son.

One day, the father saw a beggar and realized that it was his missing child. Fearing that he would lose him again, he ordered his servants to chase after him. The beggar saw these people running after him, so he became frightened and ran away as fast as he could. When the servants finally caught him, he thought that they were from the police. "I haven't done anything wrong," he cried out. "I haven't stolen anything! Why are you arresting me?"

Even though the beggar struggled and protested, the rich man's servants hauled him back to the house. When they arrived, the beggar had fainted, so the rich man had someone splash water on him to wake him up, and then he helplessly let him go.

After the beggar left, the rich man had someone follow him to find out what kind of life he had. The elder then changed into dirty clothes and smeared dirt on his face too. Carrying a broom and a dustpan, he followed the beggar and patiently made friends with him. One day, after they had quite gotten to know each other, the rich man made a suggestion to the beggar. "You work so hard every day begging for food. Sometimes you have one meal and sometimes you don't get any. Why don't you come and work where I'm working? You won't need to beg, and you can live and eat very comfortably." The beggar happily accepted.

The rich man told him what to do, and the beggar worked happily every day. No matter how heavy or difficult the job was, he was always happy and worked hard.

After a long time, the rich man was quite old. As he approached the end of his life, he saw that his son was a good, industrious person, so he announced to all that the beggar was really his own son and that all his property would belong to him.

When the former beggar heard this, he was overwhelmed. "I had nothing. How come I suddenly have so much?"

Actually, he was the son of a rich family and all the property rightfully belonged to him. It was just because he wanted to fool around one day that he became lost and had to live such a difficult life.

For so many years, the son didn't know about the grief and suffering in his father's heart. Is this any different from our own lost hearts? Every one of us has a pure nature like Buddha. We have great knowledge and wisdom, and yet many people prefer to dwell in the common world. So don't underestimate yourself!

Sundari's Slander

Sundari was a prostitute. She heard that many people followed Buddha and became monks, and among them were some of her former lovers. So she was quite resentful towards Buddha and the monks. Several other religious groups hired her to destroy the order of monks by using her beauty to seduce the monks.

However, all the monks were strict followers of the precepts. Under Buddha's wise, compassionate teaching, no one ever broke the precepts. Although Sundari tried all her charms, she was unable to tempt any of the monks. She finally hit on a shameful plan: she pretended to be pregnant, and she went around crying that a Buddhist monk had raped her. She spread the rumor everywhere, wanting everyone to think that the monks were anything but pure. The rumor spread throughout the city and soon reached the palace. Then even the king knew that the situation had become serious.

After some time, these religious groups feared that Sundari couldn't keep up the pretense forever, so they killed her and spread the rumor that the monks had done it out of rage. The seriousness of the situation had escalated to such a degree that the king immediately ordered a thorough investigation. Finally the whole truth came out and the Buddhist order was vindicated.

When the truth was publicized, the rumormongers were extremely ashamed of themselves, because they had just heard the rumor and passed it along, so that everyone suspected Buddha and his monks. Even the king felt that he had misunderstood Buddha, so the king and all the people went to Buddha and asked for forgiveness.

"I don't blame you," Buddha said to them. "I can only blame myself for having planted the cause in a previous life and thus getting this result now." So they all asked him, "What did you do?"

Buddha then told about his relationship with Sundari in a previous life. "A long, long time ago, a prostitute knew a certain businessman. They would meet and stroll in the countryside outside the city. In this area, there was a monk who was doing moral cultivation in a grass hut that he had built himself. One day, the monk went into the city, so the prostitute and the businessman went into the hut. They had a quarrel. The businessman killed her and buried her body near the hut.

"The rumor spread that the monk had raped the woman and then killed her. When the king heard the news, he commanded that the monk be arrested and executed. The businessman heard about this and he felt extremely ashamed. After a great deal of inner struggle, he decided to confess to the crime. The king then released the monk and executed the businessman."

"That woman was Sundari, and I was the businessman," Buddha concluded. "That was evil karma that I created eons ago when I was a common person in the world. Because of that bad karma, I encounter her in each life and whenever I'm successful, she always slanders me. The cause that I planted in the past creates this kind of result."

After everyone heard this story about Buddha's previous life and the resulting slander and false accusations, they all became fully aware. When Buddha was alive, all the difficulties that he encountered tell us that each person receives good or bad results from the good or bad things he or she did in the past. Everything that happens to us today may have something to do with our past lives. Everything that we do today may have effects in our future lives. Therefore, we must be extremely careful about our own words and actions.

A Snake Saves Lives

In the early years of the Chinese Republic, there was a monk named Miao Lien who lived in the Tzuyun Temple on Changchounan Mountain, Fukien Province. At eighty years of age, he was still quite healthy. He often preached to the local people about compassion, the Buddhist law of cause and effect, and the prohibition against killing. All those, young and old, who heard the monk believed his teachings whole-heartedly. The temple held a three-day service on the first and the fifteenth of every lunar month, and this monk always gave the sermons. On these days, the temple was always full of people who came to hear him.

Master Miao Lien walked on the mountain every morning, rain or shine. One day, he saw a six-foot snake. Its head and tail were bleeding and the snake was dying.

The master compassionately decided to heal the snake. He brought over some herbs, ground them and spread them on the snake's head and tail. He then went back to the temple. When he went back to see the snake the next day, it was gone.

Half a month later, the monk was preaching when a snake suddenly crawled into the temple. Although the people were frightened, no one harmed it. The monk saw that it was the same snake he had saved before, so he said to the crowd, "There's no need to fear, just let it come in."

The snake's wounds were healed. It crawled to the monk, curled itself up and raised its head, looking at the master with gratitude.

The snake seemed to understand the sermon. When it was over, it crawled out. After that, whenever there was a service in the temple, the snake would come to listen to the old monk preach. When the monk talked about the prohibition against killing, the snake seemed to understand.

One year, an epidemic suddenly spread through the area. The symptoms were thirst and high fever. All medicines were useless and many people died. No one knew what to do. Master Miao Lien and his disciples visited many sick people, but they couldn't cure them either. Heartsick and frightened, the people could only watch each other die.

One day, the snake brought some herbs to the monk. It raised its head and looked at him, as if it wanted to say something. The monk examined the herbs and discovered that all of them were for reducing fever. He gave them to the sick, and when the sick boiled the herbs and drank the soup, they were cured.

The monk then collected the same kinds of herbs and ground and dried them. The product became the famous Changchou "Monk Medicine," which saved a great number of people.

Master Miao Lien loved and cared for all living beings, not only human beings, but even insects, fish, birds and animals. Because he compassionately saved that snake and moved its heart, "Monk Medicine" was created and saved many lives.

All creatures have buddha-nature and great love. The snake was a good example. I hope that everyone can love and care for all living things, and not just human beings. We must respect even the tiniest creatures, such as ants.

Compassionately caring for all life will bring good fortune. When you kill or harm any creature, suffering will certainly result. I ask all of you to be attentive at all times.